FLOSSIE TEACAKES' GUIDE TO

ENGLISH PAPER PIECING

Exploring the Fussy-Cut World of Precision Patchwork

| FLORENCE KNAPP |

The Quilting company

fw a content + ecommerce company

www.fwcommunity.com

22 21 20 19 18   5 4 3

Email: enquiries@fwmedia.com

SRN: R4765

ISBN 13: 978-1-4402-4792-7

Editorial Director: Kerry Bogert

Editor: Jodi Butler

Technical Editor: Debra Fehr Greenway

Art Director: Ashlee Wadeson

Cover & Interior Designer: Pamela Norman

Illustrator: Florence Knapp

Photographer: Roddy Paine

Dedication

This book is dedicated to my family, who fill my heart and head with good things and who are my greatest cheerleaders in both life and book writing: Ian, Matilda, Finn, Kathyrn, Laura, Mum and Dad. I love you.

contents

INTRODUCTION

When I explain English paper piecing to someone who doesn't make things with their hands, I'm often struck, despite their enthusiasm, by an awareness of how curious it is to spend hours cutting up pieces of fabric, only to sew them together again in a different form. And to then not even retain all those carefully placed papers!

In that moment of objective clarity, I realize that EPP may seem an inexplicable and illogical activity that borders on lunacy! However, that self-consciousness is fleeting. The planning, cutting, wrapping, and stitching involved in EPP are so absorbing that I quickly find myself re-ensconced in a cocoon of creativity, order, and quiet industry.

The geometric shapes synonymous with EPP are like the pieces of a jigsaw onto which you can impose your own picture. It's a puzzle many of us feel drawn to return to over and over, enthralled by its endless potential for alternative configuration.

The addition of fussy-cutting offers yet another means to manipulate the appearance of the piecing. It's a technique that requires a fiddly perfectionism, but rewards us with the emergence of mesmerizing kaleidoscopes when the carefully cut pieces are placed in repeat.

English paper piecing is inherently portable, which makes it an activity that may spill over into the fabric of our day. EPP becomes a backdrop to watching films, talking over tea, day trips to the beach, long train journeys, or waiting for a child at lessons. It is a silent companion, equally capable of being the kite in the breeze or the anchor in a storm.

When I was invited to write a book about English paper piecing, my hope was to extend a hand—albeit a paper one—to those keen on learning the techniques required. However, in the years since I was first captivated by this form of traditional quiltmaking, I have come to appreciate English paper piecing as far more than just a utilitarian patchwork technique. So much so that it would have felt like telling only half a story to confine myself to sharing only techniques and patterns. Over the following pages, with newcomers and old hands alike, I hope to explore some of the life, history, meaning, and inspiration with which these simple fabric-wrapped papers are so often infused. These are the elements that, to me, dance around the edges of English paper piecing, giving it both its vibrancy and its draw.

Whether you read this book from cover to cover or dip in and out, I hope that these pages offer something to leave you feeling energized and reaching for a small stack of fabric and a confetti of paper shapes.

Florence

English paper piecing (EPP) is a traditional method of handpiecing used to create patchworks. By wrapping paper templates with fabric, complex shapes and intricate designs, which would be almost impossible to tackle on a machine, can be sewn together with ease. Once pieced together, the paper is removed.

| CHAPTER ONE |

THE WORLD OF ENGLISH PAPER PIECING

SINCE DISCOVERING English paper piecing, I've found it has slowly crept into more aspects of my life than I could have imagined. Its methodical processes and repetitive stitches have become my daily meditation. I find myself looking for pattern inspiration everywhere, noticing drain covers, floor tiles, and door plates. Its quiet portability has allowed creativity to spill into passages of time that would once have lain fallow.

As I have cut paper shapes, wrapped fabric around them, and then carefully sewn them together, my mind has often whirled with questions. Why do we delight in seeing things made at miniature scale? What draws us to symmetry and repeating patterns? Why is fabric-related terminology so deeply woven into the English language?

Ideas about the psychology of working with our hands also began to whisper at the periphery of my time spent paper piecing. I had a sense that creating small-scale order with these wrapped fabric shapes might somehow make the larger, less easily tamed aspects of life feel more manageable. I pondered if,

when we choose to sew by hand, as well as the simple enjoyment of making a quilt, we're also instinctively engaging in something that's fundamentally good for us. And sometimes I considered the opposite and questioned why so many of us feel compelled to keep our hands in perpetual motion!

I've cast my net to take in the work of psychologists, neurologists, mathematicians, physicists, quilt historians, and fellow quiltmakers, to discover what evidence, if any, underpins these thoughts that may be familiar to many of us who work with our hands.

I've also gathered a feast of inspiration that may be enjoyed once the needle is put down for the day. In this chapter, we'll go on a day trip to the home of a renowned EPPer, the late Lucy Boston; discover the quilts of Albert Small through his granddaughter, Liz; discuss the novel, *The Last Runaway* with author Tracy Chevalier; and learn about Fine Cell Work, an English charitable organization that takes stitching into prisons.

First though, we'll begin at the beginning, with a brief history of English paper piecing. ★

a BRIEF HISTORY

I ALWAYS BELIEVED that quilts were histori- cally made for reasons of practicality and thrift and that it is only recently, in our centrally heated homes, that we have had the luxury of turning quiltmaking into an art or leisure activity. While that assumption is true of quiltmaking in general, in the case of English paper piecing, this isn't the case at all. Since its inception, English paper piecing is thought to have been an activity of the more gentrified and educated classes because of its time-consuming nature and use of more complex geometric shapes.

The 1718 Coverlet is the oldest known paper pieced quilt top in the British Isles, and several of the more geometric blocks it contains are typical of English paper piecing. Its histori- cal relevance alone makes it breathtaking, but it's also an exceptionally beautiful and highly accomplished piece in its own right. Poignantly, we know nothing of its maker, only that the quilt bears the initials EH.

When studying older quilts, we can feel a startling imbalance between seeing the maker's hand in the now-fragile stitches, while at the same time knowing little about his or her life. A shared passion gives us a sense of affinity with the maker, but it comes juxtaposed with a sense of disconnect that she is simultaneously so unknowable.

We must often rely on clues for informa- tion. Sometimes the clues are overt—as in a quilt of hexagons that is made from the snippets of nineteenth-century dresses. In this case, from the quality and patterning of the fabrics used, quilt historians can make assumptions about the background of the quiltmaker and her family, such as how trav-

Opposite: The 1718 Coverlet is the oldest known paper pieced quilt top in the British Isles. *Image courtesy of The Quilters' Guild Collection.*

Above: Patchwork Bedcover 1860-1880. Donated by Mrs. W A Smith. *Image courtesy of the York Museums Trust (York Museum Castle).*

Above: The Miniature Hexagons Quilt above was made by
Prudence Jeffery in 1857 during a six-month sea voyage
from Liverpool to Melbourne, Australia. Measuring 72"
× 72" (183 cm × 183 cm), this stunning masterpiece was
made with ¼" (6 mm) hexagons, created in keeping with
the English style of the day, where the design radiates out
from the center. Collection of Janene Ford, Melbourne.
Photo courtesy of National Gallery of Victoria.

As people began to move around the globe
in the first half of the nineteenth century,
so too did English paper piecing.

eled, wealthy, and stylish they may have been.

Fragments of writing are also often found on the paper pieces left inside unquilted coverlets. Occasionally, these are personal snippets of a love letter or poem. Often though, they are more utilitarian—envelopes, recycled shopping lists, children's handwriting practice. Paper was once at such a premium that English paper piecers carefully repurposed it.

Other times, the clues are more subtle and taken on inference. When I studied the Lugley House Coverlet held by the Quilter's Guild in York, I was mesmerized by Catherine Eldridge's tiny stitches. They are consistent across the vast quilt of $^5/_8$" (1.5 cm) hexagons, and when counted equated to around 27 stitches per inch! The neat, painstaking perfection of her work caused my imagination to draw all sorts of conclusions about her nature.

Initially, English paper pieced designs primarily featured squares and half-square triangles. But starting around 1790, the hexagon and other more complex shapes began to commonly appear. Quilt historian Bridget Long attributes this to an improvement in girls' education as well as the wider availability of geometry primers, such as C. Hutton's charmingly titled *The Compendious Measurer (1786)*. Patterns could also be bought from tradesmen who drew up designs for ladies' work.

While we now tend to use quilting cottons and fine lawns in our English paper piecing, historically a far broader range of fabrics were used. Velvets, upholstery fabrics, fine silks, and dress cottons were mixed together with masterful abandon and a lack of intimidation around tackling more bulky seam allowances! Although shades fade at varying rates and once-vibrant yellows will often have faded altogether from an older quilt, the colors of these fabrics often surprise me by appearing no less rich than those we see today.

As people began to move around the globe in the first half of the nineteenth century, so, too, did English paper piecing. British officials began taking their families out to the colonies and their many quilts accompanied them. These women's continued practice of English paper piecing in a strange new land must have offered a much-needed connection with home.

However, examples of English paper piecing are not entirely confined to affluent women. In the 1820s, prison reformer Elizabeth Fry identified English paper piecing's ability to provide spiritual nourishment to female prisoners. It also acquired some popularity among soldiers and sailors, offering an engaging way to perfect the needlework skills required for their work, relieve boredom, or pass the hours for those convalescing. ★

FABRIC AND LANGUAGE

| Why is the fabric of our language interwoven with so many sewing-related references? |

*T*HE ENGLISH LANGUAGE is so rich with fabric-related terminology that it's hard to summarize this idea without making a clichéd reference about them being interwoven. It's perhaps telling that in Latin, both *text* and *textiles* share the same root word *texere*, meaning "to weave."

Indeed, fabric is so deeply rooted in our culture and society, it peppers everyday conversation. We talk about hanging on "by a thread," the "fabric" of society, "embroidering" the truth, a "close-knit" community, "spinning" a tale, the "thread" of a storyline, "patching up" a relationship, "weaving" a web of lies, someone "unravelling" at the seams, and "piecing together" events. We use this textile-based imagery knowing it will convey our meaning *and* be universally understood.

While the relatively breakable lone thread is often used to represent fragility, the cross-hatching of warp and weft strands, which are interwoven to form a rich and varied cloth, can represent individual elements that have come together to form a unified whole. We may not think about metaphors pertaining to the structure and construction of fabric in such an objective way on a daily basis, but over time they have become woven into our psyche to produce a language rich with visual imagery.

However, I don't believe fabric has crept into our language solely because it is a wonderful vehicle for metaphor. Thinking back to man's earliest times, aside from water, food, and shelter, fabric in one form or another was the only other true essential, albeit in the form of animal skins. Our need to cover ourselves in fabric is an instinctive one that has stayed with us all through the ages, eventually materializing in clothing and quilts.

Later, its use played another tangible role at a formative stage of our language and phraseology. The first edition of the King James Bible, for example, and many that followed were printed on pages made from durable, high-

> Fabric is so deeply rooted in our culture and society, it peppers everyday conversation.

quality cotton linen rag paper. In the 1800s, fabric and thread continued to have a physical presence as books were routinely covered in cloth and their spines bound with stitches.

Historically, people's lives were so inextricably linked with "making" that it's unsurprising the terminology used in their labors crept into the lexicon and filtered down through generations, giving our language roots, color, and a rich sense of history. For example, we talk about being "on tenterhooks" when we feel tense, which references the hooks that linen or wool was stretched on to prevent shrinkage as it dried. We say that a parent and child with similar personalities are "cut from the same cloth," referring to tailors using the same roll of fabric when making a suit to avoid inconsistencies. A traditional English nursery rhyme, still sung in playgrounds today, ends "pop goes the weasel," which refers to the spinner's yarn winder, known as the weasel, making a popping noise when it had measured out the correct amount of thread. In the American South, the phrase "in high cotton" is used to imply that life is easy because the cotton had grown so tall the picker didn't need to bend down.

Discussing these ideas around fabric and language with my mother one evening, she suggested our reverence for fabric can also be traced back to the story of Adam and Eve in the garden of Eden. Immediately upon eating the forbidden apple they "knew that they were naked; and they sewed fig leaves together, and made themselves aprons" in an attempt to cover both themselves and in turn their shame. I wonder if the symbolism of this story has become wedged in our collective psyche over thousands of years to give fabric and its ability to conceal a greater significance in our lives than we can imagine.

That textiles and the paraphernalia around their manufacture have been such a mainstay in our lives physically, spiritually, culturally, and vocationally seems to have put them at the very core of our being when developing our language. Our historical relationship causes these references to whirl around us in our modern daily lives without our even noticing their presence, so ingrained are they in our speech. Its deep-seated presence is evident in this quote from the physicist Richard Feynman, who even when discussing nature herself (for Feynman talks about nature as a female embodiment) used almost entirely textile-related words to describe her: "Nature uses only the longest threads to weave her patterns, so each small piece of her fabric reveals the organization of the entire tapestry."

Taking the prefix "im-" to mean "not," we can draw our conclusion about the importance with which we endow fabric by looking at the very existence of the word *immaterial*, which in its most literal translation suggests that if something is not material, it's irrelevant and without substance. As one who is obsessed by fabric, at times I'm almost inclined to agree! ★

WORKING WITH OUR HANDS

| What are the positive effects of handsewing on our physical and mental well-being? |

WHEN I WAS eight, my adored maternal grandmother gave me a sewing basket for Christmas. Lined in red satin, it contained pins with shiny pearlized heads, a rainbow of cotton threads and embroidery flosses, and an array of neatly packaged needles. As that year drew to a close, my grandmother and I sat quietly on her leather Chesterfield sofa while she taught me embroidery. We created petals using lazy daisy stitch and flower heads from dense clusters of French knots. I've long since forgotten those embroidery skills, but what I have retained is the memory of the calm contentment that washed over me as I tried to perfect my stitches that day. It was a feeling of absorption and peace entirely different from anything else I'd experienced.

As an adult, instinct has told me that needlework offers a myriad of benefits for mind, body, and spirit. And while researching this book I've enjoyed discovering that those instincts aren't just "Florencisms" built entirely on my own beliefs and conversations with others. Rather, they are ideas substantiated in a wealth of studies conducted by researchers, psychologists, and neuroscientists that offer fascinating insights into why sewing might make us feel so good!

In 1995, Robert H. Reiner conducted a clinical study in the Department of Psychiatry at the New York University Medical Center with fifteen novice sewists and fifteen experienced sewists. Researchers monitored the women's stress indicators, including heart rate, blood pressure, and perspiration, while they performed a range of typically relaxing activities. These involved reading a newspaper, painting at an easel, playing a solo card game, using a handheld games console, and sewing a simple pattern on a pillow. The results revealed that the heart rates of the sewists dropped by as much as eleven beats per minute, with similarly significant drops in blood pressure. Conversely, heart rates actually increased across the other four activities. Even Reiner seemed mystified by the difference in results. It's been suggested that perhaps it is the soothing, repetitive rhythm of sewing, which occupational therapist Marian Scheinholtz compares to the experience of rocking in a rocking chair.

Rhythm and repetitive movement have indeed already been shown to increase the release of serotonin in the brains of animals, lowering stress levels as a consequence. I'd always believed the sight of a rocking gorilla at the zoo was indicative of an animal at the point of a critical mental breakdown. And while that may be true, its repetitive movement is also an act of self-preservation. Researchers have found that farm animals that engage in this kind of coping strategy develop fewer stress ulcers than more passive animals. In the context of humans and English paper piecing, everything from cutting papers to wrapping pieces and whipstitching them together seems to offer an endless stream of repetitive movement with which to lower stress levels.

However, the mental space one enters into when absorbed by sewing may also play an important role in understanding its benefits. Sewists commonly talk of the "meditative quality" of sewing, asserting that with their eyes open and needle in hand, they're able to gain the same sense of calm and grounding associated with meditation. This idea is reflected in a study of more than three thousand knitters conducted by Betsan Corkhill in conjunction with the Royal United Hospital in Bath. From the study, Betsan concluded that knitting enables a much wider cross-section of society to experience the benefits of meditation because it doesn't require a person to actively understand or accept the practice itself, it just offers these benefits as a natural side effect.

The Hungarian psychologist Mihaly Csikszentmihalyi believes that this meditative state induced while working with our hands can more accurately be described as "flow," which he defines as "a state of joy, creativity, and total involvement, in which problems seem to disappear and there is an exhilarating feeling of transcendence."

According to Mihaly, when someone is completely immersed in skilled creative endeavours they can become temporarily divorced from their identity and body, due to so few of the brain's resources being left over for monitoring thirst, hunger, or tiredness. I've experienced this, having lost count of those times when I've barely noticed it's grown dark until I find myself unable to see my stitches or haven't felt hungry despite having forgotten to eat lunch or dinner. This also offers an insight into why many have successfully used needlecrafts as a way of managing chronic pain. Presumably the brain's ability to pick up on pain signals is diminished for these same reasons.

Mihaly believes that regularly being engaged in a state of "flow" is the key to human happiness. His writing suggests that while we may experience "pleasure" in certain activities—eating, sleeping, resting—it's actually "enjoyment" that allows us to reach a place of lasting happiness. He suggests that enjoyment requires us to go beyond our own basic programming in order to experience it. The key ingredients are that it stretches or challenges us, brings new experiences, or makes us feel a subsequent sense of achievement.

The neuroscientist Kelly Lambert takes this one step further, believing that through working with our hands we have the potential to fend off or lift depression and other mental health issues, often with more efficacy than pharmaceutical drugs, such as antidepressants.

Kelly found there is a critical link between the symptoms of depression and the key areas of the brain involved with motivation, pleasure, movement, and thought. She discusses how the areas of the brain that control these components form a circuit, which when activated by complex movement and intricate thought, offers a sense of well-being. She calls this the "effort-driven rewards circuit."

What constitutes an effort-driven reward then? Basically anything that elicits a sense of satisfaction derived from physical effort and focused thought to produce a tangible or visible result. Needlework certainly fulfills these criteria, although equally housework or cleaning could serve the purpose. However, it is critical that the physicality involves the hands because their movement actually activates larger areas of the brain's complex cortex than moving far larger parts of the body, such as the legs or spine.

In our modern world, where machines wash our clothes and clean our dishes, we've removed ourselves from many of the repetitive physical tasks that we would have once carried out with our hands. Interestingly, in line with this, rates of depression have risen. One study found that those born after 1970 were ten times more likely to suffer major depression than those born prior in the 1930s.

Although I am grateful that we no longer have to wring clothes through a wringer, it

> "What did you trade the minutes of your life for? Hopefully it was happiness."
>
> — Mark Lacas, CEO of Dataprism, as cited in *The Distraction Trap: How to Focus in a Digital World* by Frances Booth

seems clear that our brains feel lost unless we replace these bygone tasks with other activities. Kelly Lambert suggests that crafts may help recharge the batteries of an emotionally drained brain. When so much in our lives is outside of our control, she says it's vital to feed the brain's sense of having control over something, however small, to increase our resilience to negative thought.

On the basis of numerous studies and research, Lambert goes so far as to say, "Engaging the effort-driven rewards circuit appears to be the equivalent of taking a preventative dose of the most powerful antidepressants— and this therapeutic intervention is free!"

Indeed, clinical psychologist Ann Futterman Collier has found a myriad of positive effects in using textile arts in therapy. Studying almost 900 women, she found that those who sew, quilt, or engage in other textile activities when upset reported greater success in changing their mood and feeling rejuvenated than women who relied on nontextile-based coping methods, such as chatting with friends, reading a book, or going for a walk.

In a culture that prizes social interaction, the accepted truth is that getting out and being with others is best for us when struggling emotionally. However, what this study seems to imply is that engaging in a hand-based craft allows the brain to perform its own repair.

Psychologist Ester Buchholz writes, "We need to unshackle aloneness from its negative position as kin to loneliness." She then goes on to say, "The relief provided by solitude, reverie, contemplation, alone, and private times is inestimable. Remember that love is not all there is to psychic well-being; work and creativity also sustain health."

BBC Radio 4 recently released the results of a study concerning rest, which points to a similar conclusion. In their survey of some 18,000 people, over two thirds of respondents said that they would like more rest. When asked which activities left them feeling rested, researchers noticed that the most frequently cited items were activities done alone.

While sewing can certainly be a social activity, it seems that it may also offer a space in which to temporarily retreat from the world, delivering us back to our loved ones energized, refreshed, and more positive. When I mentioned earlier that Mihaly Csikszentmihalyi believes that the ego temporarily disappears during flow, what I didn't mention was that he also believes that when we emerge from a flow state, the ego returns with a new sense of self-confidence and self-assurance! Simply by engaging in absorbing activities, like English paper piecing, we're actually able to positively alter our state of mind and self-perception. ★

CREATING ORDER IN CHAOS

Above: Handpieced bedcover and drapes by Anna Margaretta Brereton. *Photo courtesy of Norfolk Museums Service (Norwich Castle Museum & Art Gallery).*

WHEN LIFE TOSSES up things that feel beyond my control, I often find that I only begin to process my thoughts when I have the opportunity to retreat to my sewing room to work on some English paper piecing. Initially, my attention is almost entirely focused on the task at hand—cutting papers, capturing perfectly uniform fussy-cuts, wrapping more challenging shapes with accuracy. There's a warmth and solace in these repetitive processes that stills my mind until I feel I have escaped both physically and mentally to a protective cocoon. Striving for perfection in these tasks becomes the only thing of any real import at that moment. This sense of everything else temporarily falling away offers relief and reassurance to the subconscious that some aspect of life, however small, is within my control and can be affected by my hands. I always think this offers greater comfort in attempting to restore equilibrium than we might initially imagine.

In fact, neuroscientist Kelly Lambert suggests that engaging in activities that involve

> *"I have an idea that the only thing which makes it possible to regard this world we live in without disgust is the beauty which now and then men create out of the chaos. The pictures they paint, the music they compose, the books they write, and the lives they lead."*
>
> — W. Somerset Maugham, *The Painted Veil*

using your hands to produce something tangible activates several key areas of the brain. Together, these form the accumbens-striatal-cortical circuit, a system that controls movement, emotion, and thought. Activating this circuit not only gives a sense of psychological satisfaction, but also helps the brain recall the feeling of being in control. Irrespective of the actual scale of that control, Kelly believes it cushions us and offers strength when dealing with the harder, bigger aspects of life that we can't regulate.

It seems that historically other quilters have also subconsciously leaned on English paper piecing in times of chaos. In 1800, Anna Margaretta Brereton lost her fourteen-year-old son, John, following the earlier deaths of four of her ten infant children. Utterly devastated and unable to function within regular society, she retreated to her room where she spent four years handsewing a project of staggering proportions. Anna Margaretta created not only a vast bedcover, but also handpieced drapes to go around every side of the bed she shared with her husband. The sheer magnitude of her undertaking, the ingenuity of her design, and the perfect execution are breathtaking. Although predominantly English paper pieced, it also displays Anna Margaretta's incredible skill in appliqué and embroidery.

Just four years earlier in 1796, almost two hundred miles north, William Tuke, a philanthropic Quaker, had opened the York Retreat. It was an institution that revolutionized the treatment of the depressed and mentally ill, offering therapeutic and humane care in the belief that patients would thrive if given beautiful surroundings and engaged in a range of absorbing activities, such as needlework. William Tuke's pioneering "moral treatment" spread across the globe and dominated mental health care practices for much of the nineteenth century. In many ways, Anna Margaretta's self-administered sewing prescription intuitively reflected this new line of thinking that was springing up around her.

The clinical psychologist Ann Futterman Collier suggests that while nonprofessional handcrafters rarely make consciously symbolic pieces, there's often an unintentional translation of the maker's feelings onto the work. In this case, it's difficult to ignore the symbolism of Anna Margaretta's quilt and bed curtains, in which I imagine she craved refuge from the reality of the world. Or that many of the shapes included were a stretched hexagon, often referred to as a "coffin." However, ultimately, I think her work represents catharsis. After spending four years in relative solitude piecing together these tiny fragments of fabric to create what was to be her magnum opus, Anna Margaretta was restored to the point of being able to rejoin the world, until her natural death in 1819. ★

THE QUILT IN THE CUPBOARD

| What can we do to help ourselves when our piecing feels worthy
only of being hidden at the back of a very dark cupboard? |

THERE ARE MANY positives to be found in handsewing. However, even within an arena that frequently causes one's heart to soar, there can be areas of struggle. We may fear we don't have enough flair with color, intuition in pairing prints, accuracy in our stitches, innovation in our design, or perseverance to finish things. Suddenly, the thing that should bring joy is the cause of mounting tension.

Thankfully, we are not alone in this nor is it an indication of our uselessness! It's part of the risk we take when choosing to put something of ourselves into a creative endeavour.

We tend to judge ourselves more harshly than others might. When I visit museums, the sight of a slight pucker or a misaligned seam only adds to a quilt's charm for me. Those imperfections are a tangible sign of human warmth and where I get the strongest sense of the quiltmaker's presence. With the distance of time, I'm able to allow myself that same generosity. I feel nothing but fondness for how visible the stitches are in my first English paper pieced quilt. However, it's easy to be critical of whatever project I'm currently working on, focusing only on the part where I feel it fails. The magnifying glass of self-criticism provides a narrow view, and everything that falls outside its lens ceases to be seen.

Logically, we realize we should embrace the imperfections and enjoy the process—but that's often easier said than done.

Bayles and Orland's book *Art & Fear* shares a study done in a ceramics class. The class was divided into two groups. One group was told they would be marked on the quantity of their output and the other on the quality, the latter being asked to produce one perfect pot. Curiously, when graded, the highest quality pots all came from the group asked to produce in great quantities. While this group had learnt from their mistakes and improved, the other group was stunted by their quest for perfection.

So by persevering in the face of difficulty (after a cup of tea), we may transmute our areas of struggle into growth and progress.

In this vein, for several years now I've been gradually amassing what I've come to think of as my "Personal Armory of Wise Words." Across every project, irrespective of whether it ends up on the wall, covering a bed, or lurking reproachfully at the back of a cupboard, I learn things that can guide me better in future projects, such as "Give the eye room to rest" and "Don't be afraid to reintroduce a print you used earlier in the project." I recall these "wise words" whenever I reach a point of struggle. Everyone's wise words will be different, depending on their preferences and the aspects they find challenging. Wise words aren't necessary for things we do intuitively!

Though I find myself starting to repeat old mistakes, I'm becoming better at guiding myself more quickly and easily to a place where I spot my mistake before it involves unpicking stitches. I try to take comfort in a project that hasn't worked out quite as I'd hoped, knowing that I can draw from it and use the experience to guide me in the future. ★

Fine Cell Work

| How can handsewing offer a chance for reformation and
the beginnings of a new life for inmates? |

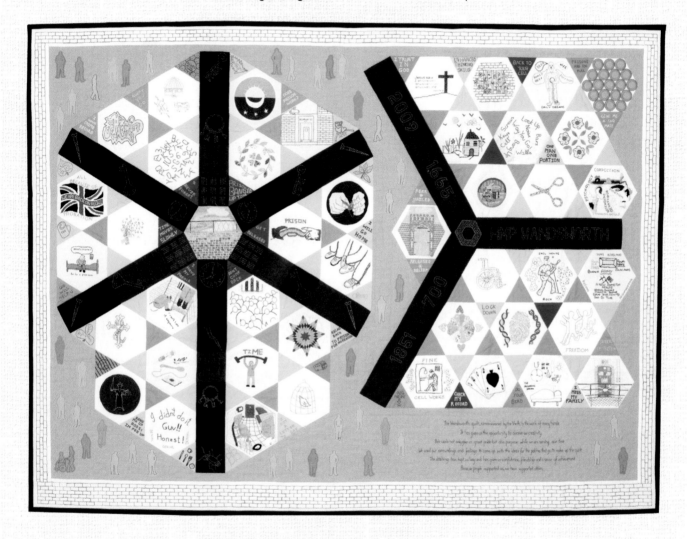

FOUNDED BY THE late aristocratic prison visitor Lady Anne Tree, Fine Cell Work is an organization that takes stitching into English and Welsh prisons. They believe that stitching offers the potential for rehabilitation as well as a myriad of other benefits to prisoners who would otherwise serve their sentence with little opportunity for personal change. This philosophy has roots stretching back to the nineteenth century when the Quaker Elizabeth Fry formed the British Ladies' Society for the Reformation of Prisoners, engaging female prisoners in patchwork during their incarceration. The female convicts aboard the *Rajah*, which set sail for Australia in 1841, were so grateful for this intervention they created an exquisite English paper pieced quilt to be sent back to the Society's founder by way of thanks. This historic relationship between needlework and prisoners is one that has been more recently rekindled by Fine Cell Work.

After decades of lobbying the government, Lady Anne Tree successfully won the right for prisoners to earn money from needlework, and in 1997, Fine Cell Work was born. Currently 97% of Fine Cell Works' stitchers are men, simply because the prison population is predominantly male. The charity sells high-quality finished pieces to an affluent and often high-profile customer base who appreciate not only the fine handiwork, but also the significance of the item, which represents the maker's self-improvement and brighter future. The fact that prisoners can be paid for their work has been critical in breaking down any stigma in prisons involving men engaging in a stereotypically female pastime. The ability to earn money and provide for their families in some small way from "inside" leads to a greater sense of self-worth and pride. For prisoners without family, it may be the only way to save for their eventual release, providing a buffer that may allow them to avoid the inevitability of returning to their old life.

Taking sewing into prisons is not without its practical hurdles: Many prisons allow inmates to be in possession of just two needles and two pins, and keeping scissors in cells would be out of the question, but the prisoners have come up with their own ingenious ways to facilitate their stitching. One Wandsworth prisoner, Sylvester, smooths his patchwork out beneath his mattress and finds that sleeping on it for a few days is almost as effective as pressing with an iron; while others deftly tear out incorrect stitches using their shaving razor's blade in place of a seam ripper.

But the benefits to the prisoners of Fine Cell Work are not only financial. The letters of thanks that prisoners receive on completing a commission for a customer have a beneficial impact on their sense of self-worth around how society perceives them. As a stitcher at Her Majesty's Prison Wandsworth eloquently explains, "it gives a feeling of positivity within this desert of negativity." The presence of needlecrafts has also changed the relationship between prison officers and prisoners. The officers begin to see the inmates in a new light, becoming interested in their work and their ability to compliment them on it goes a long way in building a rapport between them, especially when the staff themselves share details of their own sewing projects. The prisoners also benefit from the relationship they develop with their Fine Cell Work tutor, one of dozens of volunteers who regularly go into prisons and share their skills.

Prisons have found that those who sew regularly are far less likely to be involved in fights. In fact, one prisoner, cited in a study by QA Research, says, "It keeps you quiet. You block out… If there's any trouble the officers know stitchers won't be involved." Vitally, it also means that fellow stitchers become close to one another, learning a new type of sociability based around a shared enthusiasm for their skills and projects, rather than crime.

Prisoners frequently spend twenty hours per day confined to their cells with very little to do. It's an isolation that provokes boredom, listlessness, and can further the disaffection they may already be feeling. The ability to pass that time sewing has done a huge amount in helping prisoners use those long

> It seems the act of sewing is capable of bringing about positive personal rehabilitation with little input from external sources.

hours productively. One prison psychologist commented that one of her charges had a lifelong problem with self-harming until joining the Fine Cell Work program. Another prisoner who previously struggled with addiction said that he no longer uses drugs, as fabric and stitching had replaced this habit with its own insistent pull—something that any handstitcher whose own mind whirls with ideas and whose own fingers itch with a longing to sew, may identify with. It seems the act of sewing is capable of bringing about positive personal rehabilitation with little input from external sources. There's just something about the mindful, meditative repetitiveness of stitching that is able to tap into the prisoner's own inner reserves to self-correct negative traits and habits. In fact, many Fine Cell Work stitchers have continued their stitching journey after their release, diversifying into areas such as curtain-making and upholstery.

In 2010, Fine Cell Work was invited to contribute a quilt to the Victoria and Albert (V&A) Museum's *Quilts 1700–2010* exhibition. Initially, there was a struggle to come up with a layout that felt suitably meaningful until Clive, a prisoner at HMP Wandsworth,

presented a design that represented the architectural footprint of the prison. Delighted by the idea, the coordinators from Fine Cell Work asked Clive to recreate it on a larger scale in time for their visit the following week. On their return, they found that it had been confiscated by a prison officer who believed it was evidence of an escape route, rather than the innocuous quilt design that it actually was!

Each of the prisoners involved with Fine Cell Work at Wandsworth prison was tasked with creating a hexagon, using patchwork, appliqué, embroidery, or needlepoint to represent their own feelings around the experience of prison life. The finished designs were then wrapped around hexagonal off-cuts of wallpaper, chosen for its weight in view of the larger-than-average hexagons, before being sewn together. I remember at the exhibition, visitors could be found crowded around the quilt for long periods as they absorbed the many different messages conveyed in the quilt—at times poignant and sad, sometimes humorous, often characterful, and always finely executed. It was one of the most memorable, arresting, and evocative quilts in the exhibition. ★

SYMMETRY and REPEATING PATTERNS

| Why are humans drawn to symmetry and repeating patterns? And how do these things manifest in our English paper piecing? |

*E*NGLISH PAPER PIECING offers a canvas on which to experiment with geometry, play with repeating patterns, and explore different symmetries. The shapes themselves and the fussy-cut fabrics they are wrapped in provide infinite possibilities, often being used to create mesmerizing English paper pieced kaleidoscopes. These pieces frequently display both reflectional and rotational symmetry—a delicious combination that is called *dihedral symmetry.*

I find myself hungry for symmetry and repeating patterns—the harmonious balance and feeling of rightness offer both a fizz of excitement and a

> { An obsession with symmetry and pattern is something that has motivated mathematicians, scientists, architects, musicians, theologians, and artists from the ancient Greeks to the modern day. }

sense of calm. For many English paper piecers, myself included, it is fascinating to decode how a pattern repeats, to absorb where lines of symmetry fall, and to look for the mathematical framework that lies beneath a design. An obsession with symmetry and pattern is something that has motivated mathematicians, scientists, architects, musicians, theologians, and artists from the ancient Greeks to the modern day. And even without a working interest in symmetry and repeating patterns, the human eye seems naturally drawn to finding it pleasing. But why?

The French poet Paul Valéry wrote, "The universe is built on a plan, the profound symmetry of which is somehow present in the inner structure of our intellect." At the root of this are our own bodies, which have an external bilateral symmetry, meaning that the left and right sides look, outwardly at least, the same.

Like the human form, nature is often similarly arranged by symmetry, seen in the crisp outline of a leaf, the patterning of a butterfly's wings, or the juicy segments of an orange. And our world is filled with less obvious examples too, such as the structure of a virus, the crystalline form of a snowflake, and even the path of the bumblebee. In his book *The Accidental Universe*, Alan Lightman discusses how the bumblebee's erratic flight is determined by its search for symmetry, as its visual system hones in on the flowers with the most even petals. Consider, too, the perfection of the hexagonal honeycomb structure bees create and it's clear what the defining feature of the bumblebees' world may be.

From perfectly proportioned palaces to elegant formal gardens or a child's idealized drawing of a double-fronted house with a door at the center and windows to either side, our world holds symmetry in high esteem. In his book *Symmetry*, David Wade claims that these kinds of architectural symmetries often symbolize "qualities of endurance and stability." He goes on to suggest that surrounding ourselves with symmetry seems to give the world a sense of harmony and order, right down to rules of social reciprocity: "treat oth-

fig. 1

fig. 2

fig. 3

ers as we ourselves would wish to be treated."

It seems that symmetry permeates every aspect of our world. But before consulting a plastic surgeon and eschewing any deviation from that which cannot be perfectly reflected or rotated forevermore, let's pause a moment. In a BBC World Service discussion on symmetry, author and mathematician, Ian Stewart, asserted "absolutely perfect symmetric design can be boring—we like a lot of symmetry, but not too much." Indeed, I m often mesmerized by a person's quirky eyebrow or the lone dimple that appears when they smile! I realized that Ian Stewart's suggestion is also true of my approach to piecing—I often use fussy-cuts that are identically placed, but within the fabric's own design there may well be some asymmetry to loosen it up. I could see this unconscious pull to introduce a small amount of asymmetry even more clearly in an English paper piecing pattern, Perpetual Spring, that I designed a few years ago, where solid fabrics were used. Here, I've revisited it as a basis for creating graphics to show three variations: symmetry, symmetry with mild disruption, and finally, symmetry being thrown out of a (nonsymmetrically placed) window.

In the first example **(Figure 1)**, I've applied a block of repeating color to each petal. It offers rotational, reflectional, and radial symmetry. But it is slightly dull, as Stewart had suggested.

The second example shows my original design **(Figure 2)**. It incorporates a small degree of asymmetry through the petal halves, which alternate opposing shades of yellow between the inner and outer rounds. Each flower can still be repeatedly rotated by 60 degrees and remain looking just as it did before it was moved, although the reflectional and radial symmetry is lost.

The final example **(Figure 3)**, although momentarily interesting, ultimately feels chaotic and unsatisfying to look at. Symmetry has left the building.

I realize my feelings about these examples suggest that I do indeed have a preference for symmetry with slight disruption to remove some of its predictability. I'm left wondering how universal this may be—perhaps your own eyes lead you to feel something quite different?

There is a wealth of design characterized by planes of symmetrical shapes and repeating patterns out in the world. If you're looking for further inspiration for your English paper piecing, I would encourage you to research the vibrant tessellating shapes found in Islamic tiled floors, the work of the Moorish artists who decorated the walls of the Alhambra Palace in Granada, Spain, and the beautiful and distinctive shape repetitions found in Penrose tiling, only divined in the latter part of the last century. A contemplative focus can be found in deciphering the patterns and subpatterns of these intricately pieced designs and a delight in reimagining them in fabric. ★

a LIFE'S WORK

| What motivates people to embark on long-term sewing projects,
and where do they find the perseverance to finish them? |

WHEN I COME across one of those few-and-far-between quilts made from a seemingly infinitesimal number of miniscule pieces, it always stops me in my tracks. As well as the obvious visual impact, it's striking to see the tangible evidence of how a person has passed the weeks, months, and years of their life, testing the limits of what they thought possible. To me, that is often as breathtaking as the quilt itself.

The road between cutting the first piece and taking the last stitch may at times feel interminably long, fraught with technical difficulty, and points along the way at which the project could falter and peter out. It makes these Herculean works all the more awe-inspiring. I wonder what might propel someone to keep going to the point of completion without losing his or her way?

Angela Lee Duckworth, a professor of psychology at the University of Pennsylvania, believes the essential characteristic of these people is grit. As part of the vast body of her research on the subject, Angela and her team studied thousands of children in Chicago's public schools, asking each to fill in a test to measure their "grittiness." They found those children who had high levels of grit were later significantly more likely to graduate—irrespective of talent, standardized achievement test scores, or family income. Angela defines grit as having passion and perseverance for very long-term goals; stamina; the ability to maintain effort and interest irrespective of failure, adversity, or plateaus in progress; living life as if it is a marathon rather than a sprint.

But what motivates someone to undertake long-term or extreme creative feats in the first place? Perhaps those with grit simply dream on a bigger scale, knowing that they have the stamina to realize those dreams? Or maybe they enjoy putting their endurance to the test?

In his book *Flow*, Mihaly Csikszentmihalyi notes that often an enjoyable experience is not one that registers as such at the time. Rather, it can be viewed as enjoyable retrospectively, rather like climbing a mountain or running a marathon, both of which offer a lasting sense of achievement.

The authors of *Wired to Create: Unraveling the Mysteries of the Creative Mind*, Scott Barry Kaufman and Caroline Gregoire, suggest that we often fall in love with a "dream of our future self," a self who meets a particular creative challenge. But they suggest that to sustain our motivation we must also love the process—the unglamorous, everyday hard work—involved in becoming that person.

Researching this book, I was fascinated to find a common trait emerging among quiltmakers who were successful in completing long-term or extreme challenges. I noticed that they seemed naturally drawn to document their daily progress to a far greater degree than others spoke of doing. Miss Leela, one of the featured Modern EPPers in chapter 2 who regularly sews with tiny ¼" (6 mm) hexagons, told me, "I record every hour spent on a piece, whether it's cutting out fabric, tacking the paper shapes, and of course the time I spend sewing them." The late Albert Small, whose awesome scope of work is detailed in

Quilt by Albert Small; 87" × 116" (221 cm × 295 cm). *Photo courtesy of the Illinois State Museum.*

the pages to come, worked in a similar way. His granddaughter, Liz Smith, happened to mention that he kept notes on everything, from the number of stitches to how many securing knots had been made in each sewing session. The research of cognitive psychologist Benjamin Harkin suggests that this might be a key factor in attaining their goals. Harkin argues that having a goal intention is often not sufficient to ensure its attainment. Rather, he found that frequently monitoring progress, and making a physical record of the results, can be the cornerstone in one's ability to persevere with the daily "chipping away" involved in reaching a goal.

And perhaps recording details in this way offers the maker reassurance that the finished piece will be imbued with a clearer sense of worth in both their own mind and in the minds of others. Miss Leela commented that

> A quilt feels like an exquisite vehicle for leaving a legacy of warmth, care, and love.

although she can't charge an amount that properly reflects the hours spent on a piece, when she sells a miniature quilt, she includes the number of hours it has taken her to make it on the label. She feels this helps people understand just how much time and love has gone into every stitch. Indeed, when nonquilters ask about a piece of my work, the main question that comes up upon realizing it was handstitched is an incredulous, How long did this take? Often, I know the answer is in the hundreds of hours, but I'm unable to guess at anything more exact. I'm now wondering if I should've been recording my time minutely and building up my own grittiness!

In the case of Albert Small, it seems that there was an element of friendly competition motivating him. When Grace McCance Snyder wrote to him in 1939 requesting the pattern for his second quilt, which contained a staggering 63,460 pieces, he generously sent her a black-and-white photograph of his masterpiece along with a hexagonal template so that she might make her own. He then set about making his third quilt with nearly double the number of hexagons, ensuring he retained the title of having made the quilt with the greatest number of pieces!

By introducing extremes to a project, such as using the smallest pieces or including the greatest number of hexagons, a quiltmaker is able to naturally reduce the number of people who would attempt to undertake a similar feat. This has the further effect of increasing their competitive motivation (either with themselves or with others) to continue with the project.

Stephen Garcia, a professor of psychology at the University of Michigan, and his colleague Avishalom Tor coined the idea of the N-effect. They found that reducing the number of competitors (N) increases competitive motivation. For example, they found that students taking an easy timed test finished significantly faster when they believed that they were competing against 10, rather than 100, students. Although as an additional factor, Stephen told me that in the case of quilting, the other quilter(s) would need to be similar in terms of ability or personal attributes to fuel a sense of competition. A quilter of greater ability is more likely to provide inspiration or provoke emulation than competition.

Competition aside, psychologist Loretta Breuning claims we are hardwired to care about the legacy we leave, and that doing so increases our happiness. At its most primitive level, this manifests in having children who will carry our DNA, but Breuning claims that we are increasingly finding myriad ways for our unique individual essence to live on. A quilt feels like an exquisite vehicle for leaving a legacy of warmth, care, and love, and the fabric choices and signature of one's stitches all serve to make it unique. It seems natural therefore that for some gritty individuals, the desire to enhance their legacy may help them to develop a niche skill to push at the boundaries of quiltmaking. ★

THE QUILTS OF ALBERT SMALL

| Who was the man behind the once record-breaking quilts that
contained hundreds of thousands of pieces? |

I WAS IMMEDIATELY struck by Liz Smith's vibrancy and warmth as we spoke over a long-distance call one Sunday afternoon. We'd arranged to discuss her late grandfather's quilts, but the tales she told of their family were as captivating and colorful as the quilts themselves. Space restrictions allow me to share only a small glimpse of their remarkable lives, but if I told you that Albert Small's daughter was still doing cartwheels at her eightieth birthday party, it may give you a flavor of the inspiring details that I'm omitting.

Albert Small arrived from England on Ellis Island in 1903, one of millions of immigrants who passed through its federal immigration station. Unbeknownst to him, his future wife, Eva,

Albert Small's first quilt containing 36,141 pieces. 84" × 102" (213 cm × 259 cm). *Photo courtesy of the Illinois State Museum.*

had arrived within months of him. Both deaf, they would later meet, marry, and settle in Illinois. Eva was a keen quilter, and Albert would often tease the ladies of her quilting group who gathered at their house that he could do better. It was a boast that ultimately inspired him to make his first quilt.

Albert's first quilt contained 36,141 hexagons measuring ½" (1.3 cm). Basing his quilt on a rudimentary initial sketch, he worked out from the center, completing the quilt in just fourteen months. Albert quickly settled into a routine to fit in his quilting. By day, he worked outdoors handling explosives at the Ottawa Silica Sand Company, a grueling job in winter, when even Albert's moustache would be frosted with ice. On finishing his shift, he would walk the ten blocks home, stopping en route at the dry-goods store to

> *Whether he was working with fabric, wood, or paint, whatever Albert Small did was at an impossibly tiny and intricate scale.*

check for new fabric arrivals. An early supper would then allow for four hours of hand-sewing every evening. Liz told me delightedly that her grandfather had "big hands and used a small needle," before going on to describe a wooden box where he stored his hexagons, compartmentalized in a rainbow of different colors. Inside the box, he also kept a daily record of details, such as how many stitches and knots had been made, how much thread had been used, and how many hexagons had been pieced. The fact that Albert's quilts have a strong geometric feel is a fitting reflection of the meticulous, orderly mind that devised and created them. However, they are also perfectly color-balanced works of art, bringing to mind beautifully woven Islamic carpets.

Within the quilting community, Albert's quilts are widely credited as being English paper pieced, although I have been unable to ascertain whether this is based on assumption or fact. However, by virtue of their containing purely hexagons, a shape synonymous with English paper piecing, I feel this book would be the poorer if I omitted one of the greatest examples of what could be achieved using the English paper piecing technique.

After the success of his first quilt Albert raised the bar, this time sewing 63,460 hexagons measuring just ½" (1.3 cm) each. In his third and final quilt, he aspired to make something that could not be bettered, sewing an incredible 123,300 hexagons together in just four years, which set a world record at the time.

After Albert's work had been featured in numerous newspapers and magazines, the family led people to believe they stored his quilts in a vault at the bank. But when visitors came, Eva would proudly bring the quilts out one at a time for viewing, carefully unfolding each from inside the pillowcases where they were stored. It was only after his death that the family bestowed them to the Illinois State Museum in Springfield, Illinois.

Albert himself was covered from neck to ankle in tattoos, many of which he had inked himself. During the 1930s, men would often visit the Small's parlor after church on Sunday afternoons for tattooing. At one point, his wife, Eva, considered getting a tattoo, but after Albert drew one purple dot on her wrist she declared that to be sufficient!

As I spoke to Liz, it became clear that whether he was working with fabric, wood, or paint, whatever Albert Small did was at an impossibly tiny and intricate scale. It's easy to wonder about nominative determinism, in which a person's life is subconsciously steered by his own name.

Liz fondly describes her grandfather as a serious man, hugely talented, and the owner of many collections from cactus plants to tropical fish. Indeed, at the time of Albert's death, in addition to the legacy of his incredible quilts, he left his family with over 1,200 salt and pepper shakers. ★

QUILT TALES

To me, a handpieced quilt feels like an entirely different entity to one sewn on a machine. Handsewing is such a portable and sociable activity that the fabric pieces naturally become a backdrop to the conversations and life that go on around them. My piecing comes together over cups of tea when people call; gathers the faint grimy scent of trains as we travel together through the English countryside; grows bigger in my lap as I wait to collect a child from after-school lessons; rests on the flip-down table of an

> "Our lives are like quilts—bits and pieces, joy and sorrow, stitched with love."
>
> — Anonymous

airplane; absorbs tears as they plop down on hearing bad news. It is a silent companion to the mundane, the highs, and the lows in my life. So much so that a quilt feels in many ways to have an almost deceptive simplicity in its finished appearance; all that it has borne witness to is now hidden in its mute fibers.

Fellow quiltmaker and featured Modern EPPer (see chapter 2) Jodi Godfrey agrees, "English paper piecing connects me to the stories of my life. Whether because it's slow, or because it mostly happens in my lounge room, with my kids and visitors, or because it can be taken away on holidays, my quilts remind me of these times." She notes how piecing draws people in, so the quilt itself becomes a part of the life story: "I love that it's so inviting. Everyone has hands, and many people that stop by for coffee offer to help, including my children. This never happened when I machine sewed my quilts."

Sometimes the fabrics themselves begin with their own stories, even before the first stitch has been taken. Ashley Kath-Bilsky, who comes from a long line of quiltmakers, writes on her blog, "I recently found a letter from my great-grandmother to my grandmother written in pencil during the Great Depression in which she mentioned how hard it was to come by cotton and material for her quilting projects. So, she was going to make a wool quilt for one of her sons. I also have some quilt tops that were projects my grandmother worked on with her mother and her sisters. I remember my mother pointing out to me material that had once been used in childhood outfits of hers or how 'that fabric came from the kitchen window curtains'."

While some quilts may repurpose fragments from treasured clothing to reveal a whole childhood laid out in hexagons, others speak more of the quilter's personal taste in fabric. In her book *The Patchworks of Lucy Boston*, Lucy's daughter-in-law, Diana, observes, "Often patchworkers have a favorite cotton print which recurs in their work repeatedly until used up; and then comes the regret that the whole bale had not been bought!" Although I was aware of repeatedly pulling particular fabrics from the drawer, until I read this I hadn't been conscious of how such a theme may run through the body of a quilter's work, unconsciously revealing a lifetime of favorites. When I analyzed my own choices, I realized they are both a reflection of those best-loved—where the color and print seems to cause a flip-flop of delight somewhere at the core of my being—and more practical favorites that have endeared themselves because they work well for the

{ She dreams of fabric
And patterns; at dawn she wakes
To stitch their childhood. }

— Laura Barber

fussy-cuts that I am endlessly chasing.

Like a handwriting analyst, I find myself drawing conclusions about the character traits behind the stitches holding together quilts in museums. I imagine that the piecer who dispenses her stitches boldly, loosely, and using just enough to hold the seam together is likely to have had a more carefree, exuberant, and happy-go-lucky approach to life. While the quiltmaker who strives for barely visible stitches, placed in such density that they rival even the strength of the surrounding fabric, is likely to have been a more cautious, anxious creature. I wish I was more like the former, but I feel too worried my piecing may come apart to risk loosening my grip on matters and attempting to remedy the revealing signature of my own plentiful stitches. But whatever one may infer from them, it seems that every quilter's stitch is unique in some small respect. Ashley Kath-Bilsky writes of her mother, "She could even identify what stitching belonged to her grandmother, her mother, and each aunt. Like the brush stroke of a great artist, she knew each person's style."

I often wonder how much emotion an inanimate object might absorb. Especially when making quilts as gifts, I feel a strong desire to hand over something that feels entirely positive and where the only thread of emotion that runs through it is of my love and good wishes for the recipient. This often happens naturally: When I'm sewing alone, memories of conversations and time spent together swirl around in my head with such intensity that I feel I have passed several hours in the recipient's company when I put down my stitching. But such intensity of thought over the entire duration of a long-term, handstitched project is rare.

The early nineteenth-century French novelist, Honoré de Balzac, once wrote, "From the manner in which a woman draws her thread at every stitch of her needlework, any other woman can surmise her thoughts." For me, this always brings to mind the image of a woman drawing up her thread with a jerky brusqueness that speaks of being in high dudgeon! In reality, I believe that any observable emotion is often quickly diffused by the very act of sewing itself. It's an activity that seems to have an almost magical ability to bring one to a place where more thoughtful contemplation and reflection is possible. As novelist and quiltmaker Tracy Chevalier told me when I interviewed her for this book, "Someone said once that you can't sew when you're angry. It's true. Sewing calms me, and forces me to focus on the moment. I think about *that* stitch, *this* piece of fabric, *that* pattern, and the rest of the world falls away." ★

CONSIDERING DISTRACTIONS

| Why do we so often choose to multitask while sewing? And why
are we so drawn to keep our hands moving at all times? |

*I*N HIS BOOK, *Hands: What We Do with Them— and Why,* the psychoanalyst Darian Leader observes that there's often an "and" when we work with our hands. "There is listening *and* doodling; knitting *and* talking, praying *and* manipulating beads. The real question here is the and."

I wonder about the "and" that so often appears in my own sewing room in the form of listening to radio programs, podcasts, audio books, or guiltily devouring a box set in days. Invariably I welcome these distractions, often feeling I've journeyed to other places or had my mind gently stretched, without ever leaving the cutting table. And perhaps sometimes a wall of noise is a relief from the thinking space generated by spending time quietly sewing.

However, in his TED talk, Mihaly Csikszentmihalyi cites television as the largest contributor to apathy, a state he suggests is in direct opposition to the idea of flow, where one is completely absorbed in one's work. I thought about how I felt after these sewing sessions where I had lost myself in back-to-back episodes while wrapping paper shapes. I may have enjoyed it but I did not feel recharged and renewed in the same way as after sewing without distractions.

In keeping with this, the neuroscientist Kelly Lambert suggests that passivity (such as the type we slump into while watching television) can negatively affect dopamine, serotonin, acetylcholine, stress hormones, and brain growth factors! It seems that combining sewing with more passive distractions could somewhat negate the positive effects of stitching. And at its root, Darian Leader queries why one activity is not enough. I wonder if it is a symptom of our modern times and our need for a constant stream of fresh input.

Looking at things from the other side, there are times when perhaps sewing itself becomes the "and." I often spend time with family, friends, or acquaintances when the "and" of my needle and thread are ever present!

Darian Leader suggests that our hands are often used to distract ourselves from the immediacy of a situation. As far back as the seventeenth century, social commentators have queried why people felt compelled to also fiddle with their gloves, fans, or snuffboxes, rather than just being with someone.

And while it may be true that we sometimes busy our hands as a way of partially removing ourselves, it can just as frequently mean we engage more deeply with others for *that* very reason. When the hands are busy in a way that legitimizes less frequent eye contact, it is often far easier to have difficult conversations or to share confidences. With heads bent and fingers engaged, conversation can ebb and flow naturally. This often leads to a more thoughtful discussion that offers time to properly absorb what has been said before contributing one's thoughts. Indeed, in the course of researching this book, I was told by several quiltmakers how conversations quickly become more personal in a room full of handstitchers. Another concurred, thinking back to when her children still lived at home: It was always when washing and drying, hands engaged, eyes not fixed upon one another's faces, that the real conversations would occur. ★

THE PATCHWORKS
OF LUCY BOSTON

| Who was the woman behind one of the most famous English paper piecing patterns? |

O N A CRISP, autumnal day, I set off on a journey to The Manor in Hemingford Grey, Cambridgeshire, where Lucy Boston sewed together many of her English paper pieced coverlets. Born in 1892, Lucy's patchworks have been widely celebrated only posthumously. In life, she was known for her Green Knowe series of children's books, which are set in a fictional house based loosely upon her own home. Her daughter-in-law, Diana Boston, is now the guardian of the quilts and keeper of Lucy's manor house, opening its doors to visitors from around the world, sharing both tales of her 900-year-old home and private viewings of Lucy's patchworks.

Since her death in 1990, Lucy's Patchwork of the Crosses quilt design has become world-famous, inspiring hundreds of replicas. As my train makes its way toward Hemingford Grey, I sew together the honeycomb pieces of a Crosses block. I had cut out the pieces the previous evening especially for my journey, with the desire for a day of total "Lucy immersion." For a person who enjoys fussy-cutting, each block offers a perfect canvas upon which to experiment and play. The four honeycomb lozenges at the center work in a round, allowing you to pick a fussy-cut that has a circular element. (In many ways, this is the kind I enjoy most because it offers the greatest opportunity for a new pattern to emerge as the fractured pieces are sewn together.) Next, there is the opportunity to use one lone fabric—perhaps one that does not play so well when put in repeat, but lifts or unifies the overall chosen color scheme. And finally, two different sets of pairs run around the outside, offering the chance to use a conversational print that reflects back on itself. The individual blocks are then set in the quilt surrounded by a border of plainer honeycombs, so you may disregard the usual need to incorporate fabrics that give the eye room to rest and go quite wild with fabric choices! It is a wonderful design in terms of both the making and the finished appearance.

Diana Boston shows me Lucy's original sketch when she was planning her intended layout for this quilt design. It is made directly on the honeycomb diagram within the A. J.

Opposite: The Patchwork of the Crosses by Lucy Boston. *Courtesy of Julia Hedgecoe.*
Above: My Patchwork of the Crosses block, sewn and photographed en route to Hemingford Grey.

Scott catalog from which Lucy bought all of her shapes for English paper piecing. It is interesting to think that as she committed the plan to paper, she was completely oblivious that her design would inspire a legion of quiltmakers for years to come. This sketch is actually a rarity as the majority of Lucy's quilt designs were planned and stored only in her mind's eye.

Lucy came to English paper piecing rather late, only falling under its spell in her fifties after repairing some shop-bought patchwork curtains. Those curtains still hang in The Manor's dining room, so frequently repatched in Lucy's time that they are now more hand-made than manufactured. Her first quilt was

> *Lucy was an incredibly social creature, who even in her nineties held regular parties and music evenings.*

created during wartime and was quite basic, made from squares sewn from a mixture of furnishing and utility fabrics, such as old dusters. But despite this, her eye for color shone through, elevating the simple beauty of this initial foray to produce a patchwork that still looks incredibly stylish today. She quickly progressed her skills and began using templates from the A. J. Scott mail-order catalog and fussy-cutting the designs of her material to create kaleidoscopes in her work. Diana Boston tells me that Lucy created these beautiful repeating cuts entirely by eye, before painstakingly cutting out each piece with scissors, sewing as she did in a time before clear plastic templates or rotary cutters.

When we pull back High Magic from the stack of coverlets that lay right-side down on a bed up on the second floor of the manor, I am awestruck: the composition, use of color, and choice of fabrics are even more spectacular in person than the photographs I've seen of this quilt. In this piece, Lucy has adapted some of the standard English paper piecing shapes found in her A. J. Scott catalog and mixed them in with more commonplace hexagons. Bypassing the ubiquitous Grandmother's Flower Garden design, Lucy's mind danced instead with visions of a star-strewn night sky. Lucy had been disappointed by the lack of life in the sections composed of octagons and squares and resolved this by embroidering small lines radiating from the center of each

square, which adds to the twinkling luminosity of the patchwork.

When viewed in isolation, it's sometimes difficult to see what would have drawn Lucy to buying particular fabrics, but her artist's eye allowed her to see a use for them that others might have overlooked. And in the context of her patchworks, they become an essential part of a whole that is entirely beautiful. In her sixties and seventies, Lucy would frequently go on fabric-buying trips to Liberty of London or the local quilting shops in Cambridgeshire and return with vast quantities of fabric. In her later years she would more often write to her niece Caroline Hemming, who was like a daughter to her, and request that she track down certain fabrics that she imagined might work for her current project.

Lucy worked on English paper piecing projects into her nineties, when her eyesight had deteriorated to the point where her sewing was undertaken more by the feel of her needle grazing the paper's edge than by sight. In a letter to Caroline Hemming, where she endearingly refers to herself as an "old crone" she lists the things which she cannot see: "the eye of the needle, the thread (if Silko), the edge of the material, the point of the needle, the stitch I have made." And then she goes on to say that in the agony of her blindness, she even sewed her dressing gown skirt into her patchwork. It is clear that while Lucy was frustrated by her deteriorating eyesight, she handled it with exceptionally good humor and an indomitable resolve that a trifling thing such as near-blindness would not curtail her sewing activities! Nor her age: one of Lucy's final coverlets involved appliquéing her piecing to a large base cloth, which necessitated standing up at a table for hours on end in order to keep the work flat while she sewed—an unwelcome task for even a more youthful seamstress. It is testament to Lucy's immense skill that one cannot detect the physical struggle that lay behind the finished quilts.

Lucy was an incredibly social creature, who even in her nineties held regular parties and music evenings. Her warmth and enthusiasm for fun drew people to her, and when her vision became too poor to thread her own needles, friends and even children from the village would stop in to pre-thread a small stack of needles for her. At other times when she was unable to source the perfect fabric, her niece and son were drafted in, drawing or block printing the design. However, despite a community-based sourcing of supplies, Diana tells me that it would have been rare for anyone to ever actually witness Lucy sewing. When I quiz her about this, she tells me that when people were around they had Lucy's complete attention and that she would have thought it rude to continue to sew in company. It seems that Lucy's quilts were a personal obsession, saved for the long winters at the unheated manor house when it was too cold to work in the garden. This could imply that they were simply a way of passing any hours spent alone, but reading her letters to her niece, Caroline Hemming, it is clear that patchwork was all-consuming at times, but that Lucy always chose to put people first. ★

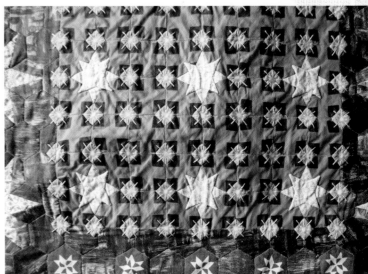

Top: Diana Boston at The Manor House, with Patchwork of the Crosses and High Magic. *Courtesy of Julia Hedgecoe.* **Bottom:** Close-up of High Magic. *Courtesy of Florence Knapp.*

THE LAST RUNAWAY

| How did novelist Tracy Chevalier find inspiration and carry out research for her book,
The Last Runaway, which has English paper piecing at its heart? |

E VEN WHEN I don't have a needle in hand, I have such enthusiasm for quiltmaking that I pore over pattern books and tomes that peel back the history of textiles. It's rare to find a work of contemporary fiction that allows this kind of book-based quilt immersion. However, *The Last Runaway* by Tracy Chevalier offers just that, a compelling story that happens to have English paper piecing woven throughout.

When protagonist Honor Bright's sister receives a marriage proposal from frontier America, the two women emigrate from Dorset, England. Once there, the main storyline revolves around Honor's involvement in the Underground Railroad, a network of routes and safe houses relied on by runaway slaves in their attempts to find freedom. Underlying that story is Honor's relationships with other women, her resentment of America, and her longing for home, which are expressed through her sewing.

Like so many English emigrants, Honor attempts to sew during the long voyage to America. As a gift, her mother had "cut out hundreds of yellow and cream cloth hexagons and paper templates for Honor to sew into rosettes." But instead of completing a Grandmother's Flower Garden quilt in the crossing, as she'd hoped, she is seasick and unable to sew. Honor finds herself dropping the hexagons overboard, knowing "they would make her sick if she ever saw that fabric again." That the sight of a fabric could pull her back to the sensations of a bobbing nausea resonated with me.

Sadly, her sister dies soon after their arrival and Honor is left in a new land, at first entirely dependent on a family who no longer have the anticipated bond of marriage to cement their relationship.

Throughout the book, Honor's resentment toward America is depicted through her amusingly unselfconscious conviction that English paper piecing and her own stitching are superior. In a letter home, she writes, "Appliqué is very popular here. To my eye it has a facile look about it, as if the maker has not thought hard but simply cut out whatever shape has taken her fancy and sewn it on to a bit of cloth. Piecing together patchwork, on the other hand, requires more consideration and accuracy; that is why I like it, though some say it is too cold and geometrical."

It's a passing incident that eventually signifies Honor's slow, unfurling willingness to embrace America, if not her husband's

Above: Tracy Chevalier and the Dovegrey Quilt at Port Eliot Festival. *Photo courtesy of Tommy Hatwell.*

family. "Bright, rich, spontaneous, Mrs Reed's quilt made the red and green appliqué quilts favored by Ohio women look childlike, and made Honor's careful patchwork contrived and overcomplicated." Near the end of the novel, it is again through quilts that the reader gets a sense that Honor's turbulent relationship with her new and estranged husband may be reconcilable. When she sees him holding their baby daughter "Honor got that feeling she had when she was sewing together patchwork pieces, and saw that they fit."

Author Tracy Chevalier is known for her 1999 bestselling novel, *Girl with a Pearl Earring*, which sold millions of copies worldwide. However, when I read *The Last Runaway*, I wondered about Tracy's quilting background and was amazed to learn that until researching her novel she'd hardly sewn more than a button on a shirt. She writes about English paper piecing with an insight that appears to draw on years of experience. There were times where I was delighted to find my own thoughts and feelings reflected back at me: "Honor loved removing the paper templates from a finished piece, a design that had been stiff and formally held in place by paper growing soft and comfortable."

In order to become well-versed in English paper piecing, Tracy took a quilting class. There she learned to make Grandmother's Flower Garden rosettes from hexagons, then pinwheels from diamonds. It was a frustrating experience. "I thought I'd go nuts. If you don't cut those diamonds or hexagons exactly right, it goes wonky. That drove me crazy. Making blocks

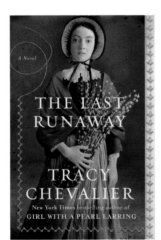

from squares and triangles, without the fiddly paper piecing, is much more forgiving. If at all possible, I prefer not to measure things."

Yet, in pinpointing what she herself disliked about English paper piecing, she was able to ascertain just what Honor may embrace. And Tracy found that the two countries' difference in quilt design worked as a useful metaphor for the problem an immigrant faces in a new country, adjusting to new styles and attitudes.

Tracy believed she would stop quilting once *The Last Runaway* was done, but it's crept into her life. She says, "Sewing calms me, and forces me to focus on the moment. I think about *that* stitch, *this* piece of fabric, *that* pattern, and the rest of the world falls away. It's a great feeling, and one we don't have enough of these days. I also like quilting because it uses a nonverbal part of my brain. So much of my life is to do with words—reading, writing, talking—and it's a relief at times to create something that I have no words for."

Tracy has also become involved at a community level. She has curated quilt shows and commissioned others, including Fine Cell Work (featured in this book), to create quilts. More recently she celebrated Charlotte Brontë's bicentenary, weaving in textile-related displays and working with the Quilters' Guild to organize the Brontë Quilt Challenge, an exhibition that later traveled to the 2016 Festival of Quilts in Birmingham.

Tracy says that there is now no doubt that quilts and sewing will remain a part of her life, but quips, "just keep me away from hexagons and I'm happy with a needle in hand!" ★

chapter two

SPOTLIGHT ON MODERN EPPERS

AROUND THE turn of the millennium, the first quilt-related blogs emerged. Later, in 2010, the photo-based social media platform, Instagram, was launched. Due to their existence, we are the first generation of quiltmakers able to immerse ourselves in a truly international online quilting community.

Not only did those first quilting blogs introduce me to kindred spirits, they also opened my eyes to an array of bright, modern fabrics. I began to place overseas orders with American patchwork stores, importing fabrics by designers such as Heather Bailey, Sandi Henderson, and Amy Butler, who were then almost unheard of in England. It wasn't long before an increased awareness of stunning new fabrics led to demand being met locally, and modern English quilting shops sprang up like daisies! I imagine this was played out around the globe.

But the online world didn't just change the face of available fabrics. It also changed the look of piecing at a more fundamental level. Where once we were confined to a small pool of inspiration, we now have access to much of the world through our screens. Ideas or interest in a particular pattern spread virally but, like a game of Telephone, the interpretation changes with each telling until something entirely new emerges. It's an environment that means our

view of quilt design is constantly reenergized and stretched. These ideas are fed back in at a local level through groups and classes, so that even those not immersed online can feel its influence.

At times, this frenetic spread of ideas can feel at odds with the slowness of our craft. The following pages offer a retreat to paper and some carefully curated inspiration. I'm privileged to share a glimpse into the lives and works of a handful of talented EPPers (those who English paper piece).

I find reading about the gentle hum and rhythm of other quilters' lives almost as enveloping as sitting down with some piecing myself. It's oddly calming to hear about the unique makeup of another person's day, knowing that at its root we have in common a feeling that our stresses dissipate when we have a needle in hand.

I was fascinated to learn about these women's motivations, inspirations, and approaches to handsewing. I hope you will be, too. I felt both recognition and delight as I came across personal similarities and differences. That there are more ways than one to skin a cat is an expression that I (and my cats) have never liked, but I can embrace the idea that there are more ways than one to piece a quilt! This chapter is testament to that.

LINDA WHITE

*L*INDA AND HER husband, Russell, live above her quilt shop, Gum Valley Patchwork, which they built on a corner of their Australian dairy farm in 2007. Beautifully church-like in appearance, the shop sits on three acres of land, surrounded by Linda's carefully tended gardens and an apple orchard with 250 trees.

Inspired by a magazine article, Linda began English paper piecing in 1978, when she was sixteen years old. For her first quilt, she cut papers from old envelopes and raided her mother and grandmother's stash of dressmaking fabrics. Eschewing school homework, she spent her evenings, weekends, and holidays sitting cross-legged on her bed, stitching. It's a quilt she still treasures today, holding, as it does, those fond memories.

Later, when her two daughters were small, she worked long days with her husband on their farm, milking cows, rearing calves, and helping with the day-to-day running. In the evenings, she would unwind by English paper piecing. People wondered how she could find it relaxing, but she says that it enabled her to "turn off and just stitch," allowing the day's pressures to quickly recede.

As Linda's skill in English paper piecing grew, her pieces became correspondingly smaller. In 2010, she began working on a Dear Prudence quilt (the original is featured in the Brief History in chapter 1) made from tiny hexagons around $5/16$" (8 mm) in size. Initially, she was wary of working at such a small scale. But after making just one flower, comprised of seven hexagons, she was hooked. From the outset, the quilt was made as a family heirloom for one of her adult daughters.

Asked about the practicalities of working at such a small scale, Linda says she first cuts fabrics into long strips, then cuts hexagons from them, thus reducing the number of smaller cuts required. She also creates her own templates for cutting fabrics, finding ready-made ones have too big a seam allowance. And while she favors glue for large pieces, for these small hexagons, she finds thread-basting to be the best choice.

Halfway through stitching Dear Prudence, Linda announced that she was going to make a second hexagon quilt for her other daughter using her own design and even smaller pieces. Although the plan was met with much eye-rolling and sighing from her husband, that second quilt was made from ¼" (6 mm) hexagons. She started at the center and worked her way out, growing the design organically and enjoying the challenge of trying to get the many borders

The award-winning Elenor Jean quilt by Linda White.

to nest perfectly together. Linda sewed 22,437 quarter-inch (6 mm) hexagons together over the course of two and a half years. It was a feat that culminated in a race to the finish line once Linda decided to enter it into the Victorian Quilters' Quilt Show in Melbourne in 2014. There, Linda's quilt won Best in Show.

Family seems to be at the center of everything that Linda does, so it's no surprise that the name of her award-winning quilt has its roots in her heritage. Her mother, Elenor, and grandmother, Elenor Jean, were the two most important and influential women in her life, so the quilt was named Elenor Jean in their honor. Linda told me, "When I was stitching Elenor Jean, she went everywhere with me… on holidays, in the car, to meetings, the dentist, on planes, trains, and buses…you name it, she was there with me!" It's a lovely thought that Linda's quilt became the embodiment of these two adored women, traveling by her side.

Follow Linda at *gumvalleypatchwork .typepad.com*. ★

JESS WILLIAMS

JESS LIVES IN the northwest of England, in Liverpool. With a once-rich industrial heritage cultivated by its port status, it is still a vibrant and diverse city today, reinvigorated by carrying the title of European City of Culture in 2008.

In the same year that Liverpool shone internationally, Jess began making a quilt, Fibonacci Fandango, that would later hang at Britain's famous Festival of Quilts. Made from 3,843 jewel-colored hexagons, Fibonacci Fandango is breathtaking in its own right, but behind its design is a deliciously intriguing story of mathematics, science, and romance.

When Jess first began to explore the idea of making a quilt featuring a spiral of hexagons, her husband pointed her toward the Fibonacci Sequence. Devised by the Italian mathematician Leonardo Fibonacci in the twelfth century, it is a series of numbers in which each number is the sum of the two preceding it. Since its inception, artists adopted it as a basis for their work due to the perfect visual proportions the sequence offers. In the case of a spiral, it is said that its use produces a "golden ratio" between each coil, which is true of Jess's Fibonacci Fandango quilt.

However, rather than limiting herself to just one perfectly proportioned spiral, Jess introduced a second spiral, working in the opposite direction. The result appears to have taken visual inspiration from the double helix of a DNA molecule, where the two strands are commonly said to "wind around one another like a twisted ladder." One strand of Jess's spiral is defined by tone (shading from light to dark), while the other is defined by color.

As for the romance element mentioned earlier, Jess created a border of hexagons interwoven with the initials "J" and "A" for her and her husband, a feature she has worked into many of her quilts. Like an optical illusion, the letters nestle seamlessly within the design until your eyes settle on them and pick them out.

With such a thoughtful structure in place, it allowed Jess to focus on what satisfies her most: melding different colors and fabrics into a harmonious whole. Indeed, the quilt's name is a nod to both the sequence on which the design is based as well as the exuberance of a Spanish courtship dance, which embodies the color and movement seen within the quilt.

In the years since its completion, the quilt has acquired even greater meaning for Jess. When a dear friend of hers died suddenly, the bereaved family asked if they might drape the Fibonacci Fandango over the coffin at her funeral service. The patchwork's abundance of joyful color would almost certainly have offered a fitting celebration of her friend's life, as well as being a visual symbol of their love and care for her as they said goodbye.

More recently, Jess has spent her time making quilts for Project Linus, an organization that distributes handmade quilts and blankets to sick or traumatized babies, children, and teenagers, with hope these tangible signs of care offer a feeling of security and comfort for the recipient. Jess uses oddments left by her quiltmaking grandmother, charity-shop finds,

and the fruits of rare, quilt shop sprees. Her piecing travels with her from her kitchen table to adventures further afield, swallowing up a little more of the stash of beautiful fabrics that she has amassed as she goes. ★

Above: Fibonacci Fandango by Jess Williams is made with 3,843 hexagons.

MISS LEELA

MISS LEELA LIVES in the Blue Mountains of Australia with her husband and their young daughter. By day, she works as an interior designer, creating beautiful homes and inspiring business spaces. In the evenings, she immerses herself in English paper piecing projects.

Leela began her English paper piecing journey thirteen years ago, when she was twenty years old. Visiting a local quilt show with her mother, she was drawn to a hexagon quilt that was being shown as a work-in-progress. Her mum, whom Leela credits with being both an incredible sewer and her craft mentor, was able to explain how it was constructed. Almost immediately, Leela bought her first packet of hexagons.

Several years later in 2009, at a quilt show in Sydney, Leela discovered miniature English paper piecing. This was the inspiration for what has now become her recognizable trademark style of tiny, impossibly neat piecing. Leela's first miniature piece was named Garden of Patience, taking 186½ hours to complete and incorporating 125 complete flowers, created entirely from quarter-inch hexagons.

Leela says that sewing in miniature relaxes her often-racing mind, soothed by the repetitive motions of tacking the hexagons and sewing them together. Piecing at such a small scale also makes a project conveniently portable—even when a piece is nearly complete, it's still small enough to be taken along in its entirety and worked on.

From a design viewpoint, Leela explains that working as a miniaturist quiltmaker means that she's able to take even a pattern intended for a large king-sized quilt and replicate it at a greatly reduced size.

As humans, we do seem to possess an almost universal fascination with viewing recognizable items in their diminutive form. From a doll's house to the more recent trend of keeping micro pigs as pets, that which was once relatively unremarkable in daily life is utterly captivating when presented in miniature.

What lies behind this fascination is difficult to pin down: Are we captivated because the scale of the item itself has been played with, or because of the secondary effect that plays with the scale of ourselves? To substantiate the latter idea, one only needs to walk around a miniature village to enjoy the curious sensation of having temporarily giant-like proportions.

Indeed, Leela herself finds joy in comparison of scale, sometimes choosing to make a quilt twice: once in miniature and once at full-size.

Leela is gratified that the niche scale of her piecing sets her work apart and delights in people's incredulity on seeing her creations. The women in her patchwork group once challenged her to see how just how tiny she could make her pieces. In response, she found herself painstakingly cutting quarter-inch hexagons down into even more minuscule diamonds and triangles. While she managed to successfully wrap and piece these tiny snippets of paper, she found the experience confirmed to her that quarter-inch finished pieces are quite small enough!

Follow Miss Leela on Instagram *@missleela_handmade*. ★

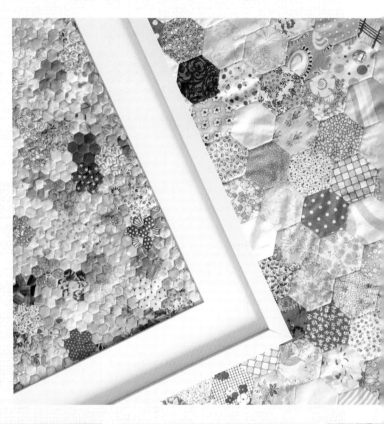

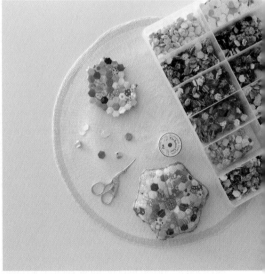

Left: Miss Leela's Wedding Medallion quilt. **Above:** Hexagon patchworks, made at two different scales, alongside carefully color-ordered storage.

DITTANY MATTHEWS

DITTANY LIVES IN Kingston, a bustling market town set by the River Thames and renowned for being one of the greenest areas in London.

Her work is characterized by a wonderful predominance of fine Tana Lawn print fabrics by Liberty of London. Dittany's love for these fabrics manifests itself not only in her quilts, but also in the photographs she regularly posts online, documenting her progress in a now-bulging notebook where she carefully catalogs and names swatches from her vast library of Liberty prints.

Although Dittany does occasionally embark on sewing up popular quilt patterns, she says she will invariably stray from the beaten path and rework the pattern to create something unique. The concentric rounds of English paper pieced stars and flowers in shades of rich blue and green Liberty prints in her One Cog Wonder began life as one of the small interlocking cogs featured in Willyne Hammerstein's iconic La Passacaglia pattern. In Dittany's incarnation, the small rosette grew and grew, with round after round being added to create what she now refers to as her One Cog Wonder.

The other noticeable flavor to influence Dittany's work is Arabic geometric patterns. Although these pieces are executed in bold, plain fabrics, which come as a stark contrast to the Liberty prints, as a body of work it remains recognizably "Dittany" because they are invariably drawn from the same jewel-colored palette of emeralds, jades, sapphires, and, occasionally, a fiery cinnabar, all shot through with flashes of white.

Although Dittany had done a little English paper piecing when she was younger, it was not until she was in her fifties, when she saw a tiled pattern, that the spark was reignited, and she felt compelled to re-create that pattern in fabric. Now, having retired, she is able to spend more time working on different projects, overseen by her cats, who are keen to appropriate any pieces that spend too long hibernating in the wings, waiting to be finished.

Follow Dittany on Instagram *@dittanym*. ★

Above: A block from Dittany's Alhambra Star.
Opposite: Dittanys One Cog Wonder, *both photographed by Catherine Pockson.*

The Influence of Arabic and Islamic Patterns

In recent years, Arabic and Islamic patterns have made more frequent appearances in quilters' work. The geometric shapes that appear in tiling, metalwork, woodwork, and carpets throughout the Middle East and north Africa offer a vast pool of inspiration for exploring the same tessellating shapes through the medium of English paper piecing. It is a practice that not only challenges one's use of color, but also one's drafting skills. While this can be done on a computer, many, like Dittany, enjoy learning the traditional geometry and drafting skills involved by using paper, pencil, ruler, and compass.

JODI GODFREY

*J*ODI LIVES ON a rural farm in Australia with her husband and their two children. Their home, shared with four other families, is surrounded by a landscape that is always verdant, save for when a crop is planted, and the green is fleetingly peeled back to reveal a rich red-brown.

As Jodi describes the patchwork of purple lucerne (alfalfa), green oats, and florescent yellow canola that is this season's backdrop, it's not difficult to imagine how this riot of colors has influenced the vibrant, richly hued array of quilts that she sews. Although when it comes to the jigsaw of shapes that appear in her quilts, it is contrastingly stark images of bathroom tiles that she credits as being a favorite source of inspiration. Jodi says that the geometric bathroom tile patterns she finds on Pinterest offer a simple, minimalist canvas onto which she can imagine her own colorful spin.

Gathering inspiration for new shapes and incorporating them into her own quilt designs is an essential component of Jodi's family-run business, creating precut paper pieces for use by quiltmakers around the world. The laser cutter built by her husband, Tim, sits on the covered veranda at their farm, gently humming as it cuts shapes from large sheets of paper. Jodi oversees its progress as she sews nearby, rising at regular intervals to sweep the pieces into tubs to later be sorted into the small envelopes made from recycled brown paper that have quickly become a familiar trademark of her business.

Inside the house, there's a different sewing project, mid-construction, beside every chair. It's a testament to the frenetic nature of Jodi's quiltmaking, which sees her frequently starting new quilts inspired by a fresh delivery of fabric, an itch to see if a design might work, or a simple loss of interest in a current project. Her willingness to hop from project to project fits in well with a life that asks her to embrace frequent interruptions as she is called upon to mediate arguments or extract a thorn from the foot of one of the farm's home-schooled children who wander in and out between tree-climbing exploits.

As a child, Jodi had a sense of missing a creative outlet in her life. She embarked on a journey to discover what that might be, throwing herself into poetry, piano, and ballet, only to be frustrated when she was unable to meet her own expectations. Later, in her post-university travels, she was struck by the beautiful, creative women she met who worked with their hands, not because they had been taught as children or were professionally trained, but simply because they enjoyed it. When she finally took up sewing, something clicked. With no previous

Above: A cozy sampling of Jodi's beautiful, vibrant quilts.

exposure to quilting, she was liberated from any sense of what might constitute "failure," and it is this that Jodi feels gave her the courage to simply play and revel in the learning process.

Jodi has gravitated toward a patchwork style that allows her mind to be at rest with a project. With an awareness that auditioning fabrics for more complex arrangements often causes her to stall, she favors a project containing just two or three repeating shapes. She's currently drawn toward using a single fabric collection, so she can delight in the colors and patterns she was first drawn to. With these self-imposed strictures in place, she can concentrate on placing color and value to change the way that a block looks, enjoying the thrill of finding ways to make a quilt sparkle, and later remembering the story of the life that went on around it as it was sewn.

Follow Jodi on Instagram *@talesofcloth*. ★

sandra cassidy

*S*ANDRA LIVES IN Broughty Ferry, which lies on the banks of the Firth of Tay in Scotland. It's a place rich in history and with a strong sense of community, where the first day of each year is celebrated with a "dook" as swimmers pile into the River Tay, breaking the frozen water with pickaxes if necessary. Sandra stays dry, offering encouragement from the harbor wall.

Having previously flitted from one creative endeavor to another, something about English paper piecing capti-vated Sandra's attention. Initially, she was so frustrated by the fiddly slowness of thread-basting the papers that she nearly abandoned it entirely. EPP's redemption came in the form of a glue pen, which sped up basting, allowing Sandra to value the slow pace of all the other processes involved in paper piecing.

Sandra says she is often inclined to try to speed through machine-pieced quilts, hoping to reach the last stitch before the momentum dissipates. But with English paper piecing, the expectation is there from the start that it will be a long process, and one that can grow as slowly as she wishes. This approach suits her life well, which is otherwise frenetic with a job and two small boys to care for. Just two shapes sewn together in time stolen here or there

is enough to satisfy her need to create and delivers a small sense of achievement. Longer chunks of time are found in the evenings while watching television, when Sandra sits on her living room sofa surrounded by small piles of paper shapes and fabrics.

Sandra's work is characterized by pieces that always feel perfectly balanced, drawing in prints from a relatively restrained color palette. Fussy-cutting is also a prominent feature. She ponders this, suggesting "fussy-cutting doesn't have to be part of EPP, although for me it now seems to have become so." Like Sandra, I think that for many of us, the two things have become inextricably linked, and we find it hard to resist that avenue of fun when presented with an array of geometric shapes.

Sandra noted that creating repetition within the design has added a whole new dimension to the process and caused her to look at fabrics and repeat patterns afresh. She tells me that she loves being able to change the look of a fabric design depending on where it is placed on the template and that she enjoys putting together designs that have a kaleidoscopic affect. She achieves this in bright, modern fabrics, often interspersed with plainer, more muted prints to deliver a feeling

of calm and visual space to the onlooker.

Follow Sandra on Instagram
@rubylovesred. ★

Above: The sparkling, crystalline elegance of a snowflake is the first thing that comes to mind when seeing this rosette by Sandra Cassidy.

SaLLY aMBeRTON

IN 2016, WHILE studying as a mature student at Winchester School of Art, Sally's work was shown at an exhibition entitled Re-Fabricate. It was through her exhibition piece, which quite literally turns English paper piecing inside-out, that Sally's work first caught my attention. Sally's quilt top didn't offer the beautiful veil of fabrics more commonly shared. Instead, it told a more intimate and revealing story, where the hand-basted hexagonal paper pieces themselves were the item on display.

Initially, Sally began making the hexagonal flowers purely for her own enjoyment. It was only when she was invited to create a piece for Re-Fabricate that she considered viewing them from a different perspective. Turned around, they served as a rueful acknowledgment that it's often the few remaining papers left inside old quilts that historians must study to uncover fragments of information about women's lives. In direct contrast to these lost histories, Sally took an active role in revealing fragments of her own story. Sally's papers were wide-ranging in source, with pieces made from diary entries, university application papers, samples of her own handwriting, and handouts from climate change presentations she had worked on.

It appealed to Sally's impish humor that when hung in the gallery space, draped against the wall and cascading onto the floor, the quilt offered only a tantalizing glimpse of its fabrics. It tickled her that this arrangement "outed" those who shared her love of fabric, as many viewers found it seemingly impossible to refrain from lifting a corner in order to see the "reverse" side.

When I initially contacted Sally, I was intrigued about whether her creation was ultimately "art" or "quilt." Delightfully, she is keen for it to be both—pleased that her piecing had the chance to be a work of art in a gallery, but now focusing on it becoming a quilt in the home. When the exhibition finally closed, Sally took several afternoon naps beneath the rustling quilt top, before removing the papers and allowing her artwork to begin the transformation into a conventional quilt offering tactile comfort. In doing so, she says that she shredded the biography that she'd fleetingly shared. This process seems to me yet further comment on the original message she sought to convey.

Sally originally learned to English paper piece at a one-day workshop and loved it right away, realizing that the act of piecing could be "mindless, mindful, or meditative." She comments that although taking a break from her textiles degree with yet more textiles may seem absurd, she found piecing hexagons relaxing, while not feeling so far removed from her studies as to cause her to feel guilt in the time it swallowed up.

Despite the kindness of her fellow students, Sally felt isolated at times as a mature student not living on campus. To counteract that feeling, she started a student stitching group called Hookers, Knitters, and Stitchers, where she taught English paper piecing and other stitching techniques with a backdrop of chatter about textiles, art, and history. Sally has since moved north, to Manchester, where she's beginning to put down roots and has embarked on the process of handquilting her hexagons.

Follow Sally on Instagram *@nbnqnbnq*. ★

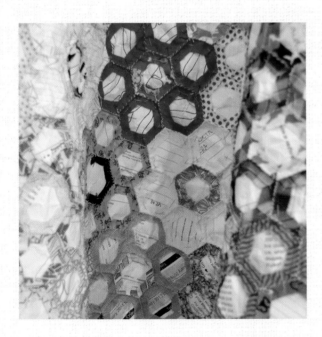

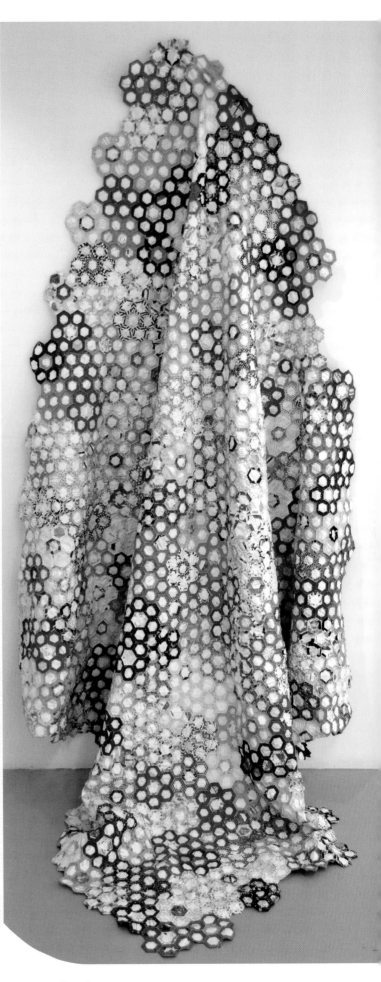

Sally's Hexagon Patchwork in the Re-Fabricate exhibition, 2016.

Lorena Uriarte

Originally from Argentina, Lorena lives in a vibrant Australian beachside suburb with her family, teaching vegetarian cookery and patchwork, and presiding over the Greater Western Sydney Modern Quilt Guild. She says that Sydney's sea and sky backdrop ebbs and flows between bright aqua blues and atmospheric stormy grays, which are also colors abundantly reflected in her fabric stash.

Lorena's vision is to make quilts that keep the eye traveling across the surface, looking for the next piece of the puzzle and revealing a new story or detail. Although it took her a while to pinpoint this as the key to her quiltmaking enjoyment, she says it's now clear that this is what fuels her love of traditionalism over stark modernism.

One of the striking aspects of Lorena's work is the frequent mix of English paper piecing with other methods, such as appliqué or traditional handpiecing. She moves nimbly between techniques depending upon what a block seems to call for, and says that as long as she's got a quarter-inch seam allowance, a variety of piecing techniques can be brought together. She finds that English paper piecing lends a reassuring promise of accuracy, especially for tight curves at a small scale.

Her enthusiasm for mixing techniques is a practice that gives her finished quilts a wonderfully varied appearance. The individual block shown here is English paper pieced, while the quilt it sits within is a happy marriage of geometric EPP and softer, often figurative, appliquéd silhouettes.

What these methods all have in common is that they shy away from offering instant gratification. Lorena tells me that she isn't interested in quick and easy techniques, preferring the challenge of a more complex design. She believes that in our frenetic fast-paced world, the results of these time-consuming projects are all the more precious.

Lorena often features fussy-cutting in her work. She enjoys finding new designs in familiar fabric by moving a set of magic mirrors (see chapter 3) across the surface to allow secondary patterns to emerge. She likens this to twisting a kaleidoscope, watching the endless swirls and lines appear. Lorena's goal is to eke out as many repeats as she can from a piece of fabric, leaving the smallest amount of scrap. However, some fabrics are much better for this than others, and she confesses that she can still revel in the self-indulgence of cutting six identical hexagons from a very large piece of fabric!

Follow Lorena on Instagram *@lorena_in_syd* and on *www.lorenauriarte.com*. ★

Above: This work in progress is entitled Blissful Abandon and is entirely English paper pieced.
Opposite: The EPP block shown is part of a quilt that incorporates many different piecing techniques.

CHAPTER THREE

INTRODUCTION TO ENGLISH PAPER PIECING TECHNIQUES

*H*AVING FEASTED on inspiring images of patchwork quilts and their stories over the previous pages, it is finally time to explore the techniques behind them. In this chapter, I will be discussing all things English paper pieced, sharing my favorite hints and tips, and demystifying the paraphernalia involved. We will cover everything from needles to fussy-cutting!

From an early age, my mother fostered in me a curious joy in finding just the right tool for a job or system for organization. I've carried this ethos into English paper piecing, enthusiastically testing new products until I've settled on the ones that enable me to work unencumbered. Any recommendations made are the result of extensive research! However, for beginners or those wishing to sew more thriftily, please don't feel disheartened by the specialty items mentioned. English paper piecing is a technique that dates back hundreds of years, and countless beautiful quilts have been skillfully created using whatever equipment was readily available or could be improvised. There is no reason why that should be any different today.

{ English paper piecing is a technique that dates back hundreds of years. }

A selection of needles
suitable for EPP.

Sewing Notions

Needles

People often find they prefer a slightly longer
needle for English paper piecing, making
appliqué or milliners needles (also known as
straw needles) a good choice.

Which needle you prefer is entirely subjective and, if you do a lot of English paper
piecing, finding the brand, length, thickness,
and type of needle that feels just right can be
something of a Goldilocks adventure. In the
same way that we might notice a particular
pen that writes nicely and seems to have a
magical ability to improve the look of our
handwriting, the same is true of a needle and
our stitches.

Look for a needle that glides through
fabric, doesn't bend too easily, rarely snaps,
has an eye that doesn't puncture your fingertip
as you sew, and can be threaded with ease.
My preference is a John James size 10 straw
needle, which is a little over 1½" (3.8 cm) in
length.

I advise choosing somewhere between a
size 9 and 11 needle for English paper piecing.
Keep in mind that needle makers are contrary
creatures who use an inverse numbering
system—a size 5 needle will be bigger than a
size 10, for example.

Appliqué needles offer a finer point, which
has the advantage of slipping between a
fabric's fibers more unobtrusively. This is a

welcome trait when sewing with a finer fabric, such as a Cotton Tana Lawn from Liberty London. However, I've found the delicacy of appliqué needles can make them more prone to snapping.

Thread

When I first began English paper piecing, I happily used any thread that was on hand (and any nearby needle, too). I'm still delighted by the first quilt I made despite its highly visible stitches. However, as my EPP journey progressed, I craved stitches that faded into the background more. Here, you can see the contrast between a thread that blends **(Figure 1)** and one that sits more visibly **(Figure 2)**.

If you prefer the look of more visible stitches, use any all-purpose thread—a contrasting color will make the stitches stand out even more. If you find the thread twists or tangles, try running it through some beeswax or Thread Heaven thread conditioner.

For barely visible stitches, use a fine yet strong thread that melts away like magic, such as Wonderfil's DecoBob or Superior Threads' Bottom Line. I find DecoBob thread to be the stronger of the two, while Bottom Line offers a greater choice of color and is more widely available. These fine threads rarely seem to tangle, and I never use wax with them. It would be expensive to invest in a new wardrobe of thread exclusively for English paper piecing, so I'd suggest initially buying just a few spools in colors that will blend well with most projects, such as white, cream, a pale silvery gray, and a mid gray. Grays have a quite magical ability to blend well with other colors!

Alternatively, pre-wound spools of thread in every color contained in a handy plastic doughnut are a wonderful option. Not only

fig. 1

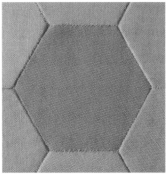

fig. 2

are they a visual treat, but the spools are handy for EPP-on-the-go and because the thread is so incredibly fine they seem to have everlasting life.

Thimbles

Although you're unlikely to use a thimble for regular English paper piecing, you may want one for sewing clamshells or appliquéing English paper piecing to a cushion or quilt. Finding a thimble that feels right may be as subjective as finding well-fitting pants! My own trial and error has brought me to a soft, malleable leather version that protects my finger while being barely noticeable. If you prefer a vegan option, I recommend investigating a metal-capped thimble made from a soft elastic material (look for one with a scalloped edge that allows the finger to breathe).

Scissors & Blades

You're likely to find yourself cutting paper pieces, plastic templates, fabrics, and thread when English paper piecing and may wish to invest in a small library of cutting instruments for each task. If you are cutting your own paper pieces, reserve a pair of scissors for paper-use only, as they will be unsuitable for cutting fabric once they have been blunted by paper. As the shapes are often small, choose a pair with fine, manageable blades. I use these same paper-cutting scissors for cutting plastic templates, too.

We'll discuss templates in more depth later, but for now, know that it's far quicker to cut fabric around a template with a small rotary cutter than to mark around it with a pen and then cut out the shape with scissors. To work with the small shapes that English paper piecing presents, I keep a 28 mm and a diminutive 18 mm rotary cutter close by. The larger is fantastic for straight edges, while the smaller of the two can be incredibly useful for cutting around curves (although for a tight inner curve, scissors may be required). You will also need a self-healing cutting mat to protect your work surface when using a rotary cutter.

Finally, you will need something to snip threads or cut into seam allowances with. While super-sharp scissors are always appealing and lovely to have in the sewing room, I'd recommend a small pair of embroidery scissors with a blunt or rounded tip that won't be capable of puncturing its way through the bag it is contained in if you take your English paper piecing on the go.

Above, left: Medium paper-cutting scissors, small paper-cutting scissors, sharp embroidery scissors, and rounded-tip embroidery scissors. **Left to right:** 18 mm rotary cutter and 28 mm rotary cutter.

Separate & Label Scissors

If, like me, you are absent-minded or have family whose own projects cause them to rifle through your sewing drawers, it's worth creating a clear system to delineate between scissors intended for cutting fabric and those for paper. The maxim of "only cut paper with red-handled scissors" is something that may stick with my children for the rest of their lives! Obviously, redness dictates my purchases in this area, to avoid throwing the entire family into scissor chaos, but that's a small price to pay for having never had a pair of my fabric-cutting scissors accidentally ruined.

Paper Pieces: the "Paper" in EPP

As the title of this section suggests, paper pieces are the essential underpinning of any EPP project. The material that you wrap around the paper shape will take on its form and become a crisp, smooth fabric version of its paper counterpart. Held in position with glue or basting stitches, the paper will remain in place until the project is finished. It offers shape and stability, as well as the delightful crinkling and rustling sounds so characteristic of any English paper piecing work in progress! Once removed, the papers can be reused if they are still in good condition or recycled, if not.

You can find all of the paper pieces for the patterns in this book at *www.quilting company.com/FlossieTeacakesTemplates*. I have also included many of the generic shapes used in EPP to give you a jumping off point for creating your own designs, which we'll cover later. (It is far less daunting than it sounds!)

However, if you'd like a paper piece of a specific size, there's a fantastic website that will generate pages of printable shapes to the dimensions of your choice free of charge. It offers hexagons, diamonds, octagons, squares, and various types of triangles. Visit incompetech.com/graphpaper.

If you don't fancy printing and cutting your own papers, you can also purchase relatively inexpensive precut paper pieces in common shapes and sizes in stores and online.

Because EPP shapes are sewn together along their edges, the only measurement you will need when buying or creating paper pieces is the intended length of a shape's side (rather than any information about diameter). Were you to buy a pack of 1" (2.5 cm) hexagons and 1" (2.5 cm) diamonds, for example, you can sew them together because the lengths of their sides are the same. These paper sizes do not include seam allowances—they refer simply to the finished size of the shapes once sewn together. We'll cover adding seam allowances to fabrics in Using Templates for Cutting Fabric, later in this chapter.

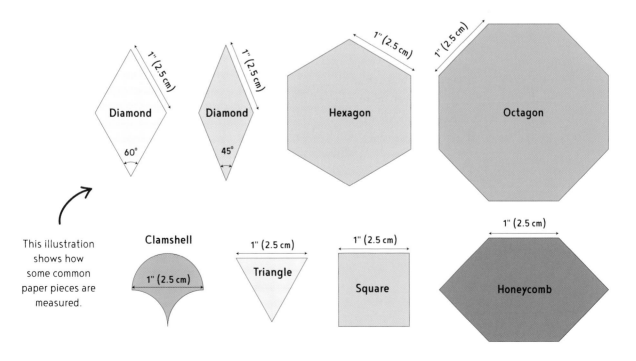

This illustration shows how some common paper pieces are measured.

Printing, Cutting & Wrapping

I tend to print paper pieces on regular paper (my ideal is 57 lb./120 gsm premium recycled paper) or very light cardstock (76 lb./160 gsm). Although cardstock isn't as malleable when piecing intricate designs, it can be a better choice when wrapping shapes that taper to a fine point and may be difficult to detect through fabric. I prefer using white paper to avoid color showing through paler fabrics while my EPP is in progress. However, as attested to by the papers found in old quilts that were cut from books, receipts, and letters, you can use anything for English paper piecing! Generally though, it's better to keep the weight of the paper consistent throughout a project.

When it comes to printing, if you are generating your own shapes, use the finest outline possible as cutting on a thick line can cause a surprising amount of inconsistency. Likewise, inaccurate cutting will have an impact on how easily your finished project fits together, so take your time.

While many shapes have a line of symmetry running through their center, a project with more complex asymmetrical shapes can become confusing if you don't work with all shapes consistently. To manage this, I wrap printed papers with the ink side facing away toward the seam allowance. This leaves visible any helpful shape lettering and keeps the ink away from the face of the fabric, as it will only touch the seam allowance. More importantly, it means that once I have wrapped all my different shapes, they will definitely fit together!

For the patterns in this book, paper pieces for asymmetrical shapes are always provided as mirror images to allow for wrapping with the printer ink on the reverse of the shape.

Above: Because of the shape's asymmetry, it's important to cover the shape so it fits correctly with the other pattern pieces once wrapped.
Below: For the patterns in this book, the ink should be visible on the reverse of a correctly wrapped shape.

tessellation:

An arrangement of shapes that fit closely together without overlapping or gaps to cover a plane in a repeating pattern.

Common Shapes

Piecing small diamonds and hexagons accurately on a sewing machine requires skill and determination, while English paper piecing lets handsewists tackle these more complex shapes with ease.

Because English paper piecing is done by sewing two sides together, it is critical the two sides are the same length and match up with the pieces placed around them so they can cover a plane without gaps. As a result, English paper piecing relies on shapes that can tessellate (see Tesselation definition below), which is why hexagons, diamonds, triangles, and squares are common in EPP. These shapes tessellate well with themselves and often with one another, making their potential for creating designs endlessly exciting and liberating!

Playing with Tessellating Designs

Here are some examples of how you can use the basic shapes provided with this book to create your own designs, from simple to complex.

A hexagon is the shape most synonymous with English paper piecing. It is frequently used alone. Here, colored hexagons have been arranged to produce what is commonly known as a simple Grandmother's Flower Garden design **(Figure 1)**.

fig. 1

It is impossible to run out of variations for hexagon quilts. With thoughtful color placement, increasingly elaborate designs can spring from a plane of humble hexagons **(Figure 2)**.

fig. 2

A hexagon can also be formed by placing three 60-degree diamonds at angles **(Figure 3)**.

fig. 3

Hexagons are laid out in a Tumbling Blocks design using the pieces shown in Figure 3 **(Figure 4)**.

fig. 4

Sewing 60-degree diamonds together can also produce a six-pointed star. The finished stars won't tessellate with one another alone, but if joined with hexagons, a pattern emerges that can repeat indefinitely **(Figure 5)**.

fig. 5

This design introduces triangles, shown in combination with hexagons and 60-degree diamonds **(Figure 6)**.

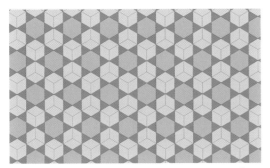

fig. 6

An eight-pointed star is formed using 45-degree diamonds. Again, these stars won't tessellate with one another alone, but by introducing squares an endlessly repeating pattern is created **(Figure 7)**.

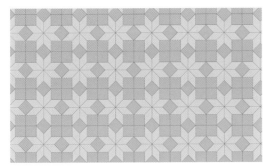

fig. 7

At first glance, this more complex-looking design appears to incorporate many shapes, but in reality it uses only 60-degree diamonds fitted together at different angles **(Figure 8)**.

fig. 8

The pattern shown here builds upon the six-pointed star design in a previous image, but this time a larger, more complex pattern is repeated. It increases the number of repeating colors that can be used and results in a more interesting design **(Figure 9)**.

fig. 9

This design gives the appearance of rounded shapes, while in reality it uses a combination of basic straight-edged shapes, including hexagons, triangles, and squares. The result brings to mind a simplified version of a traditional Wedding Ring design **(Figure 10)**.

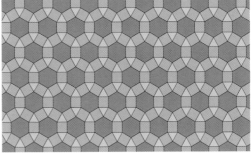

fig. 10

Above: Using a homemade clear plastic template.

Using Templates for Cutting Fabric

One of the lovely things about English paper piecing is that the paper stabilizes the fabric so you don't have to worry about the grain of the fabric.

Fabric must be cut with an added seam allowance for wrapping around the paper pieces. So a fabric shape should be cut ¼" (6 mm) bigger on all sides than its paper counterpart.

In theory, adding the seam allowance can be done roughly by eye. However, with paler fabrics, the faint outline of seam allowances may be visible through a finished quilt top.

I tend to cut fabrics with consistent seam allowances, so that if their impression is apparent, it's consistent and doesn't look messy. For this, we must embrace the world of templates!

Ready-made metal, plastic, and acrylic templates are widely available in shapes commonly used in EPP. I prefer acrylic templates because they aren't as susceptible to damage by rotary cutting as metal (you may find that metal templates damage your rotary cutting blade if you happen to veer into one while cutting). Templates tend to be available with a ¼" (6 mm) or ⅜" (1 cm) seam allowance, so keep this in mind if you have a preference for your sewing.

Above: Using a homemade clear plastic template.

Templates with cutouts that clearly show which part of the fabric design will be visible on the sewn shape are super. However, templates with a solid center are easier to hold down safely when rotary cutting around them.

I rely almost exclusively on homemade plastic templates as they offer the most flexibility. They can also be quickly remade if misplaced, lend themselves well to fussy-cutting, and are inexpensive! The one downside is that you need to be more careful with the rotary cutter to avoid shaving slivers of plastic off when cutting fabric.

Making Plastic Templates

It's easy to make your own templates using widely-available template plastic.

1 Place a paper template beneath the plastic and trace carefully over the lines **(Figure 1)**.

2 For straight edges, use an acrylic quilting ruler or grid to quickly and easily add a ¼" (6 mm) seam allowance **(Figure 2)**. For curves, make little dots at various points ¼" (6 mm) out from the outline to create the seam allowance **(Figure 3)**.

3 Link the dots up as smoothly as possible **(Figure 4)**. Cut out the template.

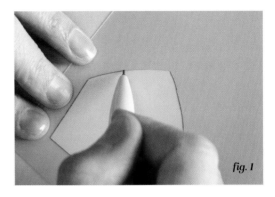

fig. 2

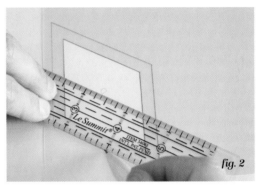

fig. 1

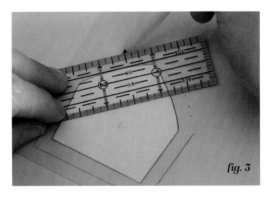

fig. 3

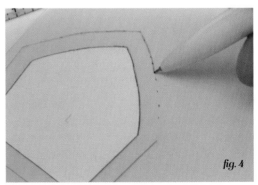

fig. 4

Basting Shapes

In order for the paper to be held securely in place while sewing shapes together, it must be basted to the fabric. Thread basting is a traditional method that has been used for hundreds of years. In fact, many EPPers find it an integral and enjoyable part of the English paper piecing process. It is possibly more environmentally friendly than glue basting, and there's less risk of seam allowances fraying when it is time to remove the papers.

Basting with Thread

Basting stitches are cut away to release the papers, so there's no need to make them neat or attractive. The method I use stitches through the paper as well as the fabric. I like the secure hold this gives, but there are many different methods, and it's all about personal preference. You can use any color of all-purpose thread, though some sewists prefer to use a high-contrast color so the threads are easily visible when it is time to cut them away.

I prefer to cut fabrics with a slightly larger seam allowance for thread basting, so I upgrade my usual ¼" (6 mm) seam allowance to almost ⅜" (1 cm). You don't need to knot your thread with this method, which makes the stitches easier to remove later.

1 Place the paper on the wrong side of the fabric (if it's a printed shape, the ink side should be facing up), leaving an even seam allowance on all sides. Stick a pin through the center to hold the fabric and paper together.

2 Pass the threaded needle through the seam allowance from the wrong side of the fabric, about ½" (1.3 cm) from one of the fabric hexagon's points, leaving a 1½" (3.8 cm) tail **(Figure 1)**.

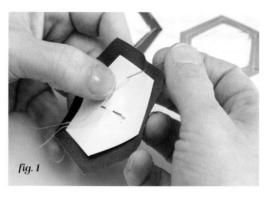
fig. 1

fig. 2

3 Referring to **Figure 2**, fold and adjust the seam allowance as shown. Push the needle through the folded seam allowance and the paper from the back, bringing the needle out on the right side of the shape.

4 Creating a stitch on the front side of the wrapped shape (large enough to remove easily later), reenter to bring your needle through the seam allowance to the right of where you initially entered (it may feel like you're working backwards) **(Figure 3)**.

5 Turn down the next seam allowance, then spear through it and the paper with your needle, before resurfacing on the previous seam allowance **(Figure 4)**.

6 Continue folding down the seam allowance on each side, surging ahead to spear it, before returning to the previous seam allowance to form a small X in each corner **(Figure 5)**. Keep the crosses relatively large so you are not left with tiny stitches on the right side of the shape, which will be harder to unpick later.

7 When each corner has a cross in it, return to the first corner and feed the needle through the seam allowance, leaving a tail of thread emerging from beneath the seam allowance **(Figure 6)**. No need to knot your thread.

fig. 3

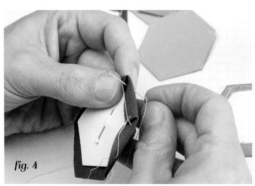

fig. 4

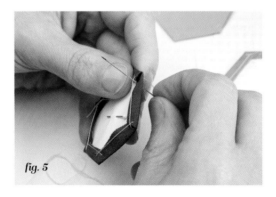

fig. 5

fig. 6

Basting with Glue

Although a traditionalist in most areas, I favor the speed of the more modern glue-basting technique. Glue-basting allows me to get to the fun of construction sooner and, in my experience, holds the pieces in place more accurately, particularly on curved edges. Although more care is needed when removing glue-basted papers, I think its advantages are worth it.

It is best to use a glue pen specifically made for English paper piecing. This fine stick of glue can be applied smoothly and accurately, is made specifically for use with fabric, and has just the right amount of tack to securely hold papers in place, while still allowing you to tease them out with minimum effort later. Glue stick refills for these pens can be bought inexpensively.

fig. 1

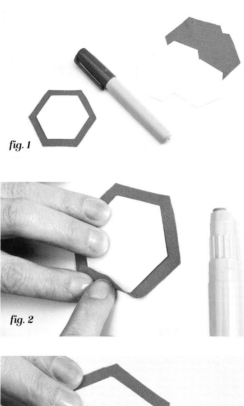

fig. 2

fig. 3

1 Simply place the paper on the wrong side of the fabric (if it's a printed shape, the ink side should be facing up at this point) **(Figure 1)**.

2 Run the glue along one side of the paper and fold the fabric in as shown, following the crisp edge of the paper **(Figure 2)**.
NOTE: *In **Figure 2**, I've used glue along the length of the shape, but it's perfectly acceptable to just put a dot of glue in each corner if you prefer. Either way, try to avoid leaving a thick layer along the very edge, as this can make sewing more difficult if it transfers into the fold of the fabric's seam allowance.*

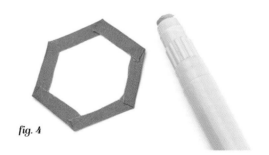

fig. 4

3 Run the glue along the next side, over the paper and any fabric that might already be folded in, then stick the next side down **(Figure 3)**. Continue until all sides are basted down **(Figure 4)**.

Wrapping Different Shapes

If you're new to English paper piecing, it can seem overwhelming imagining how each shape might be wrapped, but it's actually much simpler than you might expect.

When wrapping a variety of different shapes, particularly diamonds or triangles, as the fabrics are folded in a "dog's ear" of material will form where the seam allowances converge. Let the dogs' ears fly free, neither cutting them off nor gluing them down, as they are necessary to stop the seam allowances from fraying onto the front of the basted shape. Simply move them to one side when sewing.

In the photos on the opposite page, I've wrapped a half dozen different shapes so you can see how they look from both the front and the back.

Also, always consider whether any of your shapes have shorter sides or two sides that taper to a finer point where they meet and it may be harder to detect where the paper piece begins or ends once they're obscured by any seam allowances that have been folded in. In that situation, it's often best to baste those sides first (see below).

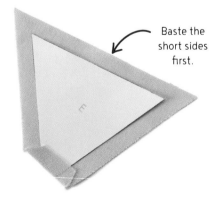

Baste the short sides first.

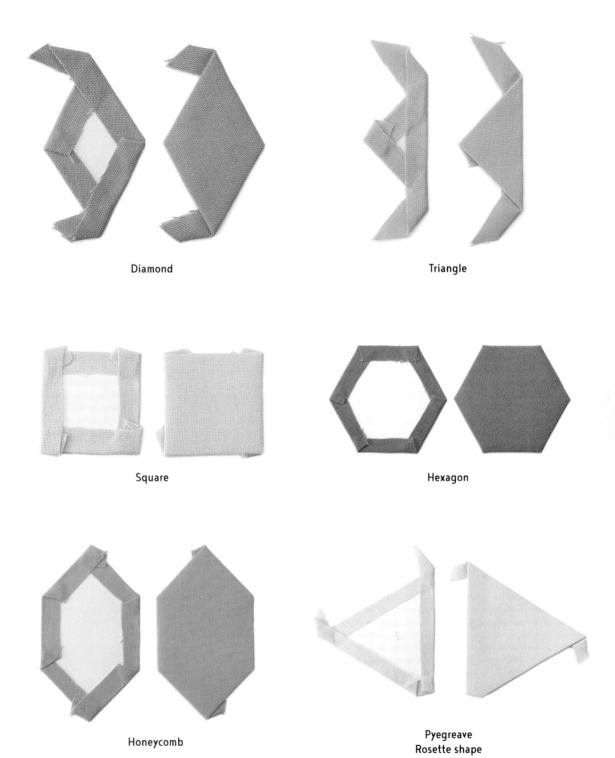

Diamond

Triangle

Square

Hexagon

Honeycomb

Pyegreave
Rosette shape

Wrapping Curves

Basting and wrapping curves is a bit different than basting straight-edged shapes. I prefer to glue-baste curves instead of thread-basting, so that's what's shown here.

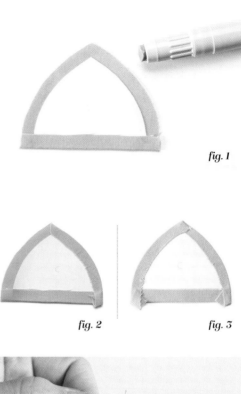

fig. 1

1 Glue down any straight edges first to hold the paper in place (Figure 1). For gentle curves like the one shown here, begin by turning the seam allowance in at the center of the curve. Using a firm finger, smooth the fabric under to each side, closely following the curve's outline (Figure 2). When basting straight edges, I sometimes use only a dab of glue at each corner. With curved edges, I apply glue to the whole of the curved edge to ensure a smooth finish that stays in place (Figure 3).

fig. 2   fig. 3

2 For less gentle curves, which often appear on the inner edge of a shape, you can make tiny snips in the seam allowance before gluing down the fabric (Figure 4). This will help the seam allowance sit smoothly (Figure 5). Just $^{1}/_{16}$" (2 mm) cuts are all that is needed to make a difference, while avoiding the risk of the cut traveling across the seam allowance and onto the face of the fabric.

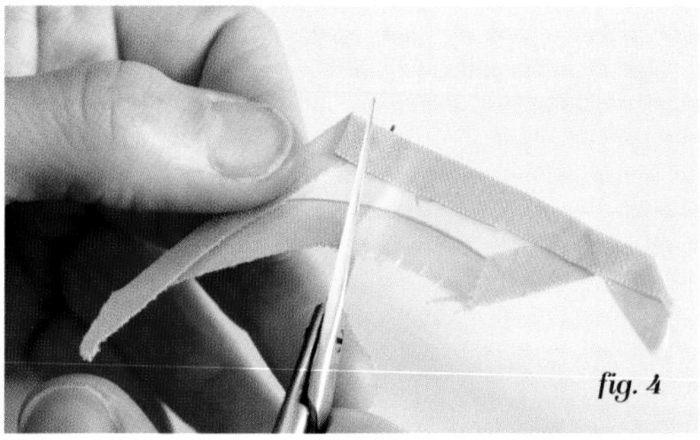

fig. 4

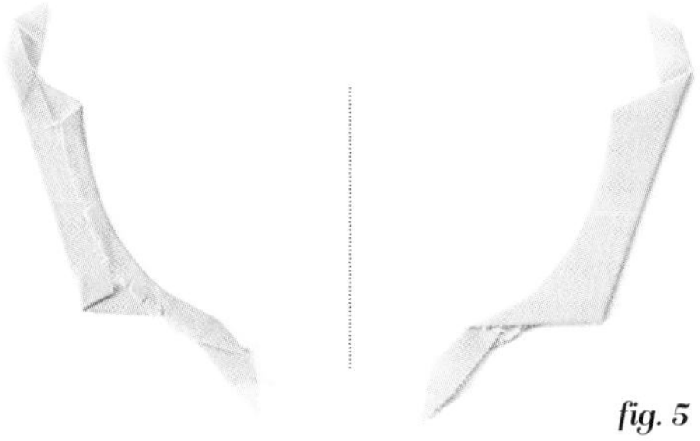

3 As with straight-edged shapes, before wrapping a curved piece, consider whether any of the shapes have fine points or very short sides where it may be harder to detect where the paper piece begins or ends once they're obscured by a folded-in seam allowance. In that situation, baste those sides first (Figure 6).

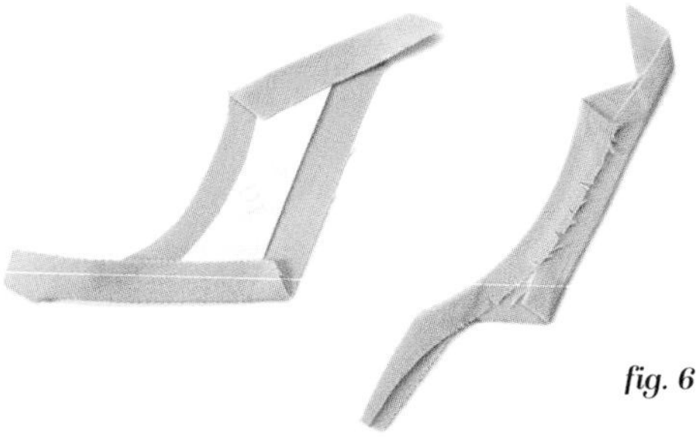

fig. 5

fig. 6

Basted Curved Shapes

Here, you can see how some curved shapes look once basted.

APPLECORE (Figure 7)

fig. 7

FLOWER (Figure 8)

fig. 8

Curves from The Ripple Effect Quilt pattern (below) **(Figures 9–10)**

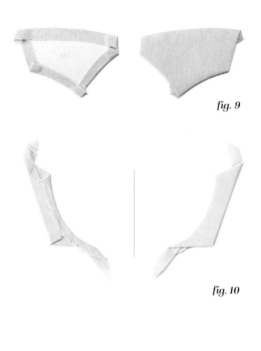

fig. 9

fig. 10

The Ripple Effect Quilt features curved shapes.

A Trick for Threading Needles

When English paper piecing, your hands can quickly tire of grasping the needle tightly to keep a fine thread in place and prevent the thread's tail from slipping the needle. To avoid what I call "rigor mortis claw grip" from setting in, I tie my thread on to the needle, so I can keep my fingers relaxed. **TIP:** *This is easier using a superfine thread, such as Bottom Line.*

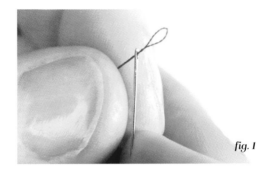

fig. 1

1 Fold a piece of thread so it has a 4" (10 cm) tail.

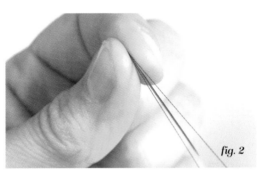

fig. 2

2 Push the head of the loop through the eye of the needle **(Figure 1)**. **TIP:** *It helps to twist the tip of the loop a little to make it narrower.*

3 Pass the loop over the sharp point of the needle **(Figure 2)**. Be sure not to let the end of the tail pass through the needle's eye.

fig. 3

4 Pull the threads to make a secure knot. The thread will be held securely on the needle until you're ready to cut it free with a small pair of scissors when you're finished sewing **(Figure 3)**.

PRODUCT TIP

Needle Threaders: If you're using a thicker thread or prefer a needle threaded up in the conventional way, you may want to explore the many ingenious needle threaders that are now on the market. Created specifically for use with handsewing needles, they can make life easier—especially if you struggle with poor eyesight.

Making a Securing Stitch

To prevent your stitches from unraveling, it's important to secure them at the beginning and end of each stitching line.

1 Place two fabric-wrapped paper pieces with right-sides together (**Figure 1**).

2 Pass your needle through the corner of two edges, catching only a few threads from the fold of each seam allowance (**Figure 2**). Draw the thread through, leaving a small tail. Repeat in the same spot (**Figure 3**). Pull the thread through until you have a small loop, then pass your needle through the loop before pulling the rest of the thread taut (**Figure 4**).

3 If desired, repeat step 2, making another stitch in exactly the same place, passing the needle through the loop again. You're now ready to start whipstitching the two edges together (see How to Whipstitch).

4 To make a securing stitch when you come to the end of a line of sewing, simply pass the needle through the loop of thread that forms when making a stitch and pull it taut. Then cut off the surplus, leaving a small tail of thread (**Figure 5**).

fig. 3

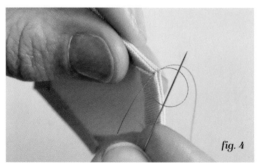

fig. 4

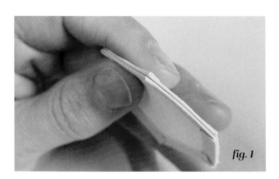

fig. 1

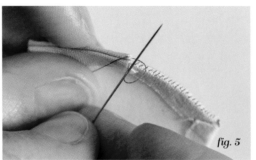

fig. 5

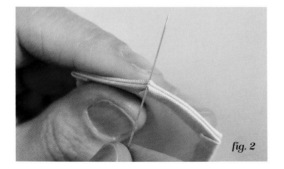

fig. 2

How to Whipstitch

When I first began English paper piecing, I briefly wondered if a ladder stitch, with its ability to completely disappear from view when joining two edges might be a better choice. However, my trials revealed that a ladder stitch isn't nearly strong enough, proving that there is sometimes a reason why things have been done the same way for hundreds of years.

NOTE: *I'm using a contrasting thread color for clarity in these photos. It is more common to choose a neutral shade or one that blends with the fabric.*

1 After making a securing stitch (see Making a Securing Stitch), enter the fabric on the opposite side of where the thread last emerged. Next, pass the needle through the fold of both fabric pieces, capturing just a few threads from each, then pull the thread all the way through **(Figure 1)**. **TIP:** *The fewer threads captured and the closer to the fold in the fabric, the less visible your stitches will be.*

2 Return to the opposite side from where the thread emerged and repeat step 2 **(Figure 2)**. The tip of your needle should always be entering the fabrics from the same side.

3 Continue joining the two sides of fabric in this way. Every ½" (1.3 cm) or so, I occasionally pass my needle through the loop of thread that forms when making each stitch to give some mid-seam security **(Figure 3)**.

4 When you reach the end of the edges you're sewing together, carefully make some securing stitches **(Figure 4)**.

{ A **whipstitch** is also known as an overcast stitch because the stitch casts over the edge of the fabric. }

NOTE: *You will find a rhythm that determines how dense your stitches are. I usually make around twenty-five stitches per inch. But as long as there are enough stitches to hold pieces together securely, any number you settle on—between ten and thirty stitches per inch—is absolutely fine.*

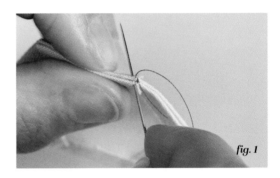
fig. 1

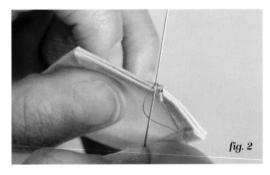
fig. 2

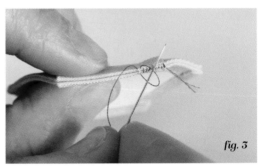
fig. 3

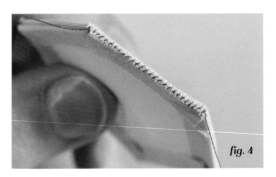
fig. 4

Sewing Straight Edges

Sewing straight edges is easy whether you're joining identical **(Figure 1)** or nonidentical shapes **(Figure 2)**. First, align the two edges to be sewn with right sides facing. Sew the pieces together from end to end, before tackling the next seam.

You may sometimes need to fold your work to join two seams—this is a perfectly normal part of English paper piecing. I advise making your folds gently though, without actively finger pressing creases into your work **(Figure 3)**.

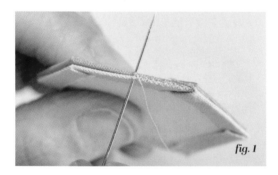

fig. 1

fig. 2

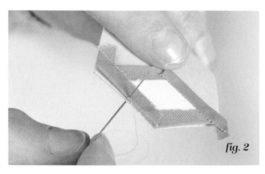

fig. 3

The Easy Way to Sew Stars

Creating stars from diamonds is a common starting point in many EPP patterns. However, if you work in the round **(Figure 4)**, it is easy to end up with an unwanted gap in the center of the star **(Figure 5)**, as you try to fit the final diamond into the nearly formed star shape.

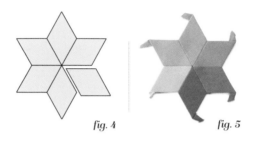

fig. 4   fig. 5

Where possible, it's best to avoid working at sharp angles. If stars are made in two halves, you can carefully align the two sides **(Figure 6)** and sew along a straight seam to join them **(Figure 7)**.

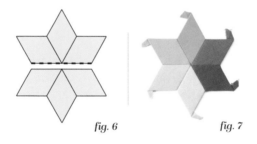

fig. 6   fig. 7

Hole or no hole, on the reverse of the star, the dogs' ears can all be swept around to fall neatly into place to leave minimum bulk on the right side **(Figure 8)**.

fig. 8

My Peony EPP that I created a few years ago includes many different types of curves.

Sewing Curves

Sewing curves can seem daunting, but once you dive in, it quickly becomes only marginally more challenging than piecing straight edges. Yes, really!

Unlike a straight edge, when you're working with a curve, you can't join the entire length of two sides in one go—just a small section at a time as you tease the edges together bit by bit. This means you can't be certain that two end points will definitely align by the time you get to the end. Some fox-like cunning is required to ensure that the end points do meet and that your seam ripper can stay in the drawer!

When you're new to this, there are two methods detailed here that can help ensure you stay in alignment over the course of a curve. Play around with them and see which works best for you. You can even combine the two if you prefer!

These methods offer reassurance and will teach you to accurately judge how two curves go together. However, with practice I think you'll find a rhythm and intuitive understanding for curves that will allow you to eventually feel confident sewing curves by eye.

Marking the Midpoint

Turn the two pieces to be joined facedown. Around the midpoint of the seam to be sewn, draw a line with a disappearing ink pen that intersects the curve across both pieces. Add additional marks if you'd like extra guidance **(Figure 1)**.

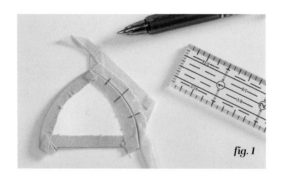

When you begin sewing, you'll have little "way markers" at various points that will signal where the two pieces should meet in order to stay in alignment **(Figure 2)**. This allows you to adjust your work to compensate or correct a problem before it becomes a larger one.

fig. 1

fig. 2

Sewing the End Points Together

For this method, simply place the pieces with right sides together. Make a few securing stitches at one end where the two end points meet. Cut the thread, then align the end points at the other end of the seam and sew a few securing stitches there **(Figure 3)**. As you travel along the seam, it will be easier to keep the shapes in alignment. Combined with marking the midpoint, this can be a really effective way to sew a curve.

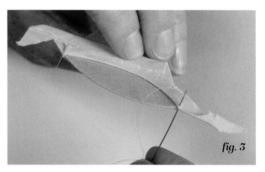

fig. 3

product tip

Pilot makes wonderful FriXion fabric pens with ink that can be easily removed with heat or friction. Note that the ink can sometimes reappear at very low temperatures, so they're best avoided if your quilt may eventually be shown in a chilly exhibition space. However, for our purposes here, ink usage is confined safely to the seam allowances.

How to Sew a Curve

1 Place the pieces right sides together, aligning the points you intend to start sewing **(Figure 1)**.

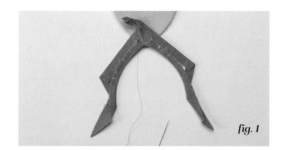

fig. 1

2 Sew up to the point where the two edges naturally diverge **(Figure 2)**.

3 Align just one section at a time, taking only a few stitches before realigning the edges.

fig. 2

4 At the center of a curve, push the pieces up slightly to allow the curved edges to form a 3-D curve together **(Figure 3)**. **TIP:** *It's easier to go with the curve, rather than fighting against it.*

fig. 3

5 Take a few securing stitches when you reach the end of the seam **(Figure 4)**.

Troubleshooting Curves

Once you've found a rhythm for curves and no longer feel the need to rely on the techniques outlined earlier, things may still occasionally go awry. Here's how to prevent yourself from being outfoxed if you find yourself in that predicament.

fig. 4

Regularly stop sewing mid-seam to double-check the end points will meet when you get to them. If it looks like they won't, take a few securing stitches wherever you've sewn up to and cut the thread. Go to the end of the seam, align the endpoints, and take a few securing stitches **(Figure 5)**. Work back up to the place where you stopped sewing, teasing the curve into place as you go. While a curve is trickier to sew, it naturally offers more flexibility than a straight edge to be teased in this way.

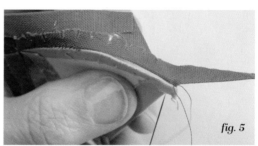

fig. 5

Sewing Curves in Sections

One last piece of advice. Before sewing curves, always check to see if a seam can be broken down into smaller sections of sewing. This is often possible when there's an obvious apex and means you can avoid sewing unnecessarily long seams where things can go awry. If you were to start sewing at the dot in **Figure 6**, for example, there's a good chance that the pieces may be out of alignment by the time you reach the end point. However, starting at the apex of the shape (the dot in **Figure 7**) provides anchorage and lets you sew each side in turn, which helps the pieces stay properly aligned.

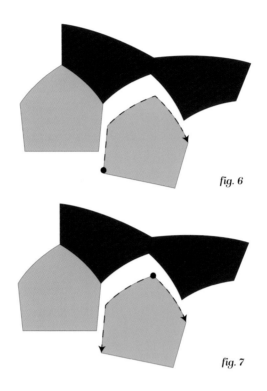

fig. 6

fig. 7

author tips

If you're struggling with any element of your EPP technique, try these tips:

- Consider if a particular tool isn't working well for you. If so, experiment with alternatives.

- Work mindfully. Notice when your work does and doesn't go as you'd hoped and look at what you did differently.

- Try out different ways of doing things. You will learn so much by experimenting.

- Share your work on social media and call on others for help. I've been the lucky recipient of many amazing tips over the years simply from voicing the things I'm struggling with.

- Don't give up because you're disappointed in the end result. Your skills will improve with every project and with the distance of time, you will barely notice the "flaws" you're focused on now.

Curious Clamshells

Clamshells are a slightly curious shape that merit a section of their own. They're used widely in English paper piecing, and while you can wrap and piece them just like any other EPP shape, most sewists reach the universal conclusion that the easiest way of tackling them is actually with a mixture of English paper piecing and appliqué. On the download that comes with this book (find the link in chapters 4 and 5), I've included paper pieces for 1½" (3.8 cm) and 4" (10 cm) clamshells. It's trickier to create accurate fabric cutting templates for clamshells, so I've included those, too. Here's how to sew clamshells:

fig. 1

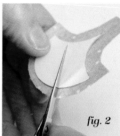

fig. 2

fig. 3

1 Cut the papers and fabric using the pieces and template on the link. For the 1½" (3.8 cm) clamshell, I like to trim a little off the top curve, about ⅛" (3 mm), to create a smaller seam allowance **(Figure 1)**. Also, I like to make small cuts into the seam allowance **(Figure 2)** to produce a smoother finish. Neither of these steps are necessary when wrapping the larger 4" (10 cm) curves.

fig. 4

2 Starting at the center, baste the top outer curve of the clamshell to the paper **(Figure 3)**, leaving the two inner curves unwrapped **(Figure 4)**. Wrap with a firm hand to give a smooth edge that follows the line of the curve right to the very tip of the shape on each side.

fig. 5

3 Place two clamshells right sides together. Disregarding the lower seam allowance, join the sides with just two to three whipstitches at the point where the tips of the papers meet **(Figure 5)**. Cut the thread.

fig. 6

4 Continue joining the clamshells together in this way until you have a row that is the required width for your project **(Figure 6)**.

fig. 7

fig. 8

fig. 9

5 Repeat this process until you have made several rows. Keep in mind that the eventual layout requires that every other row will have one extra clamshell in it. (For example, the number of clamshells per row will alternate: four, five, four, five, and so on). Press and remove the papers **(Figure 7)**.

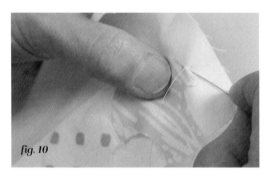

fig. 10

6 Apply appliqué glue to the folded seam allowance of the first row of clamshells **(Figure 8)**. Place the top row of clamshells on a strip of fabric (I chose a white cotton as I didn't want it to show through my lighter-colored clamshells) that is a little wider (about ½" [1.3 cm]) than the widest row of clamshells and roughly twice the height of that row of clamshells **(Figure 9)**. **TIP:** *I like to finger press a horizontal halfway line in the strip before placing the clamshells to help with placement. They can sit at rather jaunty angles until brought under control.*

fig. 11

7 Appliqué the folded curve of the clamshells to the fabric, catching just a few threads from the top edge of the shape **(Figure 10)**.

fig. 12

8 Place the second row on top of the first. Align the rows so the top of the outer curve in the bottom row rests at the point where two clamshells join in the top row. Baste in place with appliqué glue, then appliqué in place **(Figure 11)**. Continue in the same way until you have the desired number of rows **(Figure 12)**.

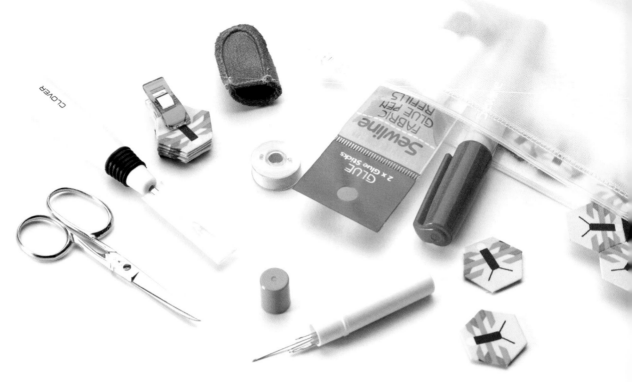

English Paper Piecing On the Go

One of the joys of English paper piecing is that it is so portable! Here are some things to consider packing before going on your way.

I like to store my English paper piecing in sturdy, clear plastic stationery pouches. They have enough form to prevent small pieces from getting bent in my handbag, and the plastic protects everything from getting wet. They're also incredibly light, and the transparency allows me to find what I want without emptying all the contents onto my lap.

Inside the pouch, I keep all the basics I might need. For me, these include needles, small curved or blunt-nosed scissors (to avoid them jabbing their way out of the pouch), a glue pen, a spool or two of thread, a thimble for any EPP related appliqué, and, as a realist, a seam ripper. And, of course, some pieces to sew together.

Empty plastic glue-pen refill packets make fantastic needle cases and offer an environmentally friendly recycling option. If you don't use glue for basting, you can purchase needle cases instead. Alternatively, a professional costumier recently introduced me to a dome threaded needle case, which holds up to ten threaded needles without tangling threads. It's quite ingenious and seems to increase workflow, as well as reducing the need to thread up needles on the go.

I feel anxious about taking a large piece of work away from the safety of my sewing room, so when I'm on the move, I prefer to break a project down into smaller sections and the component parts will only be assembled into something larger once home. It also ensures that it remains a portable pastime—rather than one where I'm trying to fit a large half-finished quilt into my handbag!

A dome threaded needle case holds up to ten threaded needles without tangling threads! The Clover Dome Threaded Needle Case, shown here, is widely available online.

Pressing Your Work

I am a huge fan of the iron and believe that good pressing can make a piece of work look infinitely more lovely and well sewn.

While you should use your own judgement to decide if you feel comfortable ironing fabric-covered paper from a safety point of view, here's how I like to do things:

I press all my fabrics before wrapping any shapes to ensure my fabric shrinks before being sewn if it's going to react to the steam. Once wrapped, I press the fabric-covered shapes before sewing them together, which stabilizes the pieces and crisps the edges. Go lightly with the steam to avoid saturating the papers.

Finally, I press the completed project again before the papers are removed. I believe this stabilizes everything and settles the pieces into their new form better than it might once the papers are removed. (I try not to use steam at this point.)

And once the papers have been removed? Yes, predictably, I press once more. Everything should definitely be nicely flattened now!

When & How to Remove Papers

I like to keep EPP papers in place until the very end of a project. I feel it protects the seams a little better and helps stabilize the pieces before they are made into a quilt or wall hanging. However, for those who wish to reuse papers throughout a project, it's fine to remove them, just remember one simple rule: Never remove a paper from a piece until it has something adjoined on each side. Once the paper has been removed from a piece of fabric, it will be more difficult to accurately whipstitch it to another piece.

To remove the papers from thread-basted shapes, you can simply snip the threads in the X with a small pair of scissors.

To remove the papers from glue-basted shapes, gently tease the seam allowance away from the paper, taking care not to fray the fabric as shown in the **Figure 1** example.

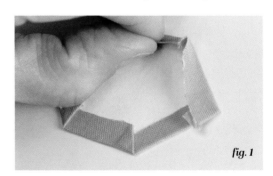

fig. 1

Appliquéing EPP to a Background Fabric

An entire English paper pieced quilt can take a year or so to complete depending on how intensively you're able to work on it, so creating a quilt combining English paper piecing with some speedier methods of construction can be an appealing proposition, particularly if you have a head bubbling with new ideas.

You might choose to appliqué a clutch of small English paper pieced rosettes across a quilt-sized background or appliqué a pieced medallion to a square of fabric and surround it with machine-stitched borders to quickly bring it up to a more usable size for a quilt! Either way, it's useful to have some basic appliqué skills. When choosing a background fabric, consider whether a darker color or an intense print may show through in areas of paler fabric. If it does show through, you can very carefully cut away the background fabric that sits behind the fabric, being careful not to cut through the piecing itself. Be sure to leave an adequate seam allowance so that the background fabric doesn't fray.

Before attempting to appliqué your English paper piecing to a background, make sure all of the papers have been removed and any loose threads that may show through paler fabric have been snipped away. If there are any dog's ears protruding, you'll need to press them with an iron at this point to ensure they lie neatly hidden beneath your work **(Figure 1)**.

TIP: *You may want to use a stiletto awl to avoid burning your fingers if it's fiddly!*

fig. 1

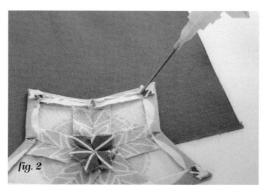

fig. 2

Smooth out the background fabric and assess exactly where you wish to place the EPP. You can secure the EPP in place using pins or basting glue (my favorite is Roxanne's Glue-Baste-It). I tend to favor appliqué glue, which I apply to the back of my work (rather than the background fabric), being careful not to saturate the fabrics or allow it to mark the front of my work **(Figure 2)**. The English paper piecing is then ready to be securely appliquéd down.

Hand-Appliqué Stitch

1 Thread an appliqué needle, matching the thread color with the piecing rather than the background color. Secure your thread. You can do this in two ways:

A) Create a knot in the tail of the thread. In the middle of one of the pieced edges, fold open the seam allowance and stick the needle into just the EPP fabric from the wrong side of the fold in the seam allowance in order to bury the knot **(Figure 1)**. **NOTE:** *If you're glue-basting, you'll need to remember to do this before sticking a shape down.*

B) With the shape glue-basted or pinned down, take a few securing stitches on the reverse of the background fabric, near one of the edges to be appliquéd, before bringing your needle out to the front of your work **(Figure 2)**.

2 Begin sewing by making a small stitch in the background fabric that reemerges almost immediately, going up through the fold in the EPP fabric **(Figure 3)**.

3 On the base cloth, opposite to where the needle just emerged from the EPP fabric, take another stitch through the background fabric. Continue making stitches in this way. **NOTE:** *I tend to make the stitches in my background fabric just inside the outline of where the EPP rests, so that the appliqué stitches will be well hidden. The stitches on the background should move along about $1/8$" (3 mm) with each stitch. The stitch in the seam allowance of the EPP fabric doesn't move the process forward, it's just to secure your work* **(Figure 4)**.

4 When you've appliquéd the outline of the entire shape, turn your work over and make a few securing stitches inside the line of stitching, taking in only the background fabric **(Figure 5)**.

fig. 1

fig. 2

fig. 3

fig. 4

fig. 5

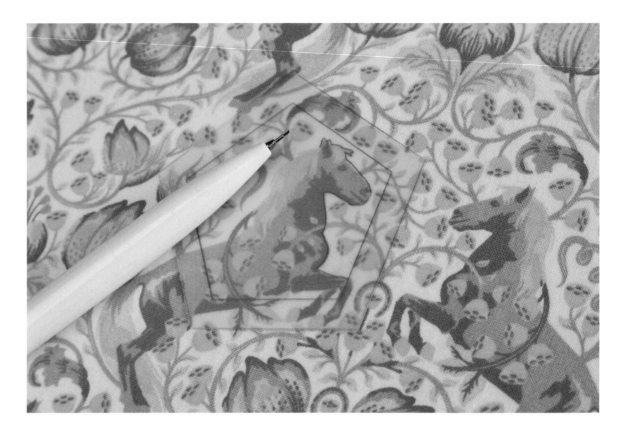

Fussy-Cutting

Despite its name, to me fussy-cutting feels like the most joyful part of English paper piecing! It opens up a whole new dimension for creativity and provides endless opportunity to stretch the artistic side of our sewing skills, as we place repeating snippets of print side by side to see unexpected patterns emerge and kaleidoscopic rosettes spring to life! It is truly exciting.

Fussy-cutting also offers new avenues for playfulness, even if that is not usually a part of your sewing personality. The skill and impressive displays that are created with fussy-cutting allow us to hide more irreverent graphics within our quilts, opening a door for some frivolity to creep in without reducing our work to something that feels childish or naïve.

The only downside to fussy-cutting is that snipping specific features from fabric can leave your stash looking like moths have ravaged through it. But this seems a small price to pay for the loveliness of what can be created!

In the following pages, I'll discuss different types of fussy-cutting, what to look for when considering which fabrics might fussy-cut well, and of course, all the techniques needed for getting your cuts perfect every time!

This fabric showing horses rearing up is an obvious example of what to look for in a conversational fabric

Fussy-Cutting:
Intentionally cutting fabric to feature a specific part of a design.

Tools for Plotting

I can be indecisive when choosing fabrics for a rosette and often try lots of options before deciding on one. Changing fabric-wrapped shapes in and out of a design can be easier if the pieces are held in place while experimenting. Securing wrapped papers to a sheet of inexpensive foam core art board with regular pins is perfect for this.

Magic Mirrors

Available at quilting shops, Magic Mirrors are made from a light, shatterproof glass and, despite their expense, are a valuable investment. Being able to see what a design may look like in repeat will save you money and the time involved in cutting out a design, only to decide it's not as pleasing as you'd hoped! Because Magic Mirrors reflect the same portion of fabric repeatedly, this works best with symmetrical prints.

To start, set a plastic template in the desired position on your fabric. Expand the mirrors, then set them on the seam allowance line of the template with the hinge on the point where a round of shapes will converge (**Figure 1**). For a more obvious visual of exactly what will be on display, make paper templates of your shape. The seam allowance will act as a frame for what you'll see (**Figure 2**).

Alternatively, you can use Magic Mirrors to preview a work in progress. Simply wrap enough paper pieces to fill one section (**Figure 3**), then place the hinge of the mirror at the centermost point, with the sides spread out to hug both sides of the fabric arrangement. This will give a good impression of what your work may look like if you cut out the rest of the pieces needed to complete the rosette (**Figure 4**).

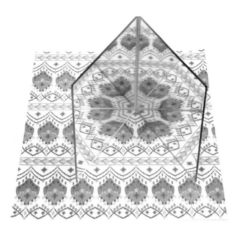

fig. 1

fig. 2

fig. 3

fig. 4

How to Fussy-Cut Fabric

For me, the one essential for fussy-cutting is clear plastic sheets for making templates that can be drawn on. (Use a pencil and you'll be able to rub out any markings and reuse the template indefinitely.) Template plastic is widely available at online quilt shops if you don't have a nearby store that stocks it.

One of the challenges of fussy-cutting is finding features that recur frequently enough to avoid buying yards and yards of fabric. Before fussy-cutting fabric, always count the number of times your desired motif appears to make sure you have enough repeats in your length of fabric to let you cut out all of the pieces you will need. You may want to also consider if there is enough distance between repeats to fit in the whole template. If there's not, you'll need to exclude the motifs that will be lost in this way from your headcount.

fig. 1

fig. 2

fig. 3

1 Create a template to match your paper piece (see Using Templates for Cutting Fabric for directions), making sure the line you initially marked denoting the paper shape is clearly visible. This will define a window, showing what you'll actually see once a shape is wrapped with fabric.

2 Place the template on your fabric and focus on the area inside the seam allowance window when choosing the part of the design you'd like to use. Whatever falls outside this line will be obscured in the seam allowance. When you've found an area that you'd like to fussy-cut, take a pencil and trace over any defining parts of the design—this will act as a guide to ensure that you have everything lined up correctly when you cut out subsequent pieces **(Figure 1)**. Cut carefully around the shape with a rotary cutter **(Figure 2)**.

3 Find a place where the chosen design repeats in the fabric, then line up the pencil drawn template to ensure you have found an exact copy. Cut the shape. Continue in this way to gather all the cuts you'll need to cover your papers.

4 Sometimes, when cutting pieces for a symmetrical or conversational design, you will need to turn the template over, so that you can cut the mirror image of the design you've marked onto the template **(Figure 3)**.

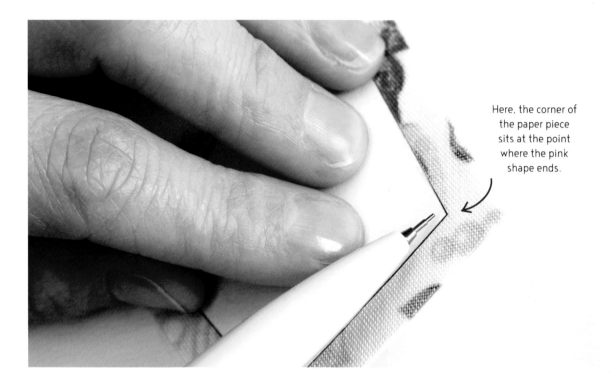

Here, the corner of the paper piece sits at the point where the pink shape ends.

Wrapping Papers with Fussy-Cut Fabric

I have been affectionately teased by sewing friends in the past for declaring something to be a "precision moment." At the risk of inciting more teasing, I feel I should declare this a precision moment.

A little extra care is required when wrapping papers with fussy-cut fabric, as painstaking cutting is easily undone by hurried wrapping. You may be surprised to discover how just a fraction of an inch or millimeter difference in wrapping can cause a design to not meet up correctly or flow together well.

When you place a paper template on the wrong side of the fabric, you'll often be able to see the outline of the design through the seam allowance—study this carefully. Notice where the corners or points of the paper shape hit certain parts of the design and make mental notes about these details, so that when you come to wrap the subsequent shapes, you're

able to align them in just the same way. Simply eyeballing an even seam allowance around the perimeter doesn't always work (due to the intrinsic fallibility of "eyeballing") or protect you against previous discrepancies made during cutting.

I like to recheck these points as I glue each side and then again once the shapes are complete. If there is a discrepancy, move the shapes around. You may find that some wrapped shapes sit adjacent to one another more happily than others, as it can take only a fractional difference in wrapping to alter things.

Fussy-Cut Patterns

Symmetrical Running Patterns

This type of fussy-cutting offers great potential for "redesigning" a fabric's print and allowing it to emerge as something completely new and unexpected! For this variety of fussy-cutting, it's necessary for the pattern pieces to run in a round with sides touching to allow the pattern to join up.

When looking for suitable fabrics, you'll need to find prints that are designed with symmetry in mind. For the pattern to flow smoothly into both of the adjacent pieces, the design will need to sit in the same place on both the left- and right-hand sides of the shape. Prints that include some form of stripe or banding often work well.

Magic Mirrors work brilliantly for assisting with this type of fussy-cutting.

  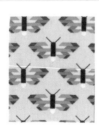  

These swatches show the fabric design before being fussy-cut and pieced.

Fractured Glass Running Patterns

As before, this type of cutting is for pieces that sit in a round with sides adjoining. There is no need to hunt for symmetry in a fabric's print, so it offers a useful way to loosen up fussy-cutting and make it appear a little more spontaneous and less precise. By focusing on a disembodied part of a print and then repeating it without caring whether lines or shapes meet up with one another when placed against adjacent pieces, a delightful new fractured pattern repeat will often emerge.

Magic Mirrors don't reflect how cuts like this will look when set against one another, but they do show a flavor of the colors and shapes you might capture. I suggest you go wild experimenting. Place the mirror randomly on the fabric at angles that are at odds with the run of the print, in order to see how many unexpected slices of color and pattern emerge.

These swatches show the fabric design before being fussy-cut and pieced.

Conversational Patterns

Like the shapes shown below from The Ripple Effect Quilt in chapter 5, many English paper piecing patterns have areas where a pair of shapes sit side by side, inviting you to create a conversational pattern (essentially a mirror image). Specific fabric is needed to allow pieces to "talk" and face one another—or face away from one another. Luckily, many fabric designers create prints with designs that either have two mirrored halves (a feature that appears facing in both directions) or identical designs that "flip" upside down in every other row.

You can also use conversational prints in the round to create a design that runs with two different lines of symmetry. However, this is only really successful if the round is made up of an even number of pieces **(Figure 1)**. A round

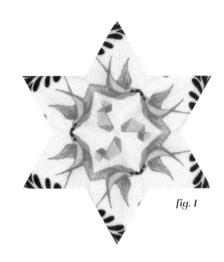

fig. 1

comprising five 72-degree diamonds would produce two pairs of happily conversing images and one lone piece, which is unlikely to be visually appealing due to its lack of symmetry.

Intentional Isolated Patterns

This type of fussy-cutting creates fewer new and unexpected patterns, but can still produce a kaleidoscopic feel because of the identical pieces being repeatedly displayed. It's a good way to showcase prints that lack symmetry, but are too lovely not to use. Sometimes, when placed in a round, this type of fussy-cut will produce the impression of a chase—demonstrated quite literally in **Figure 1**, where the dog is chasing its own tail! You don't have to stick to showing just one isolated feature though. In **Figure 2**, a bowl and spoons alternate to give the impression of a table laid for a simple feast.

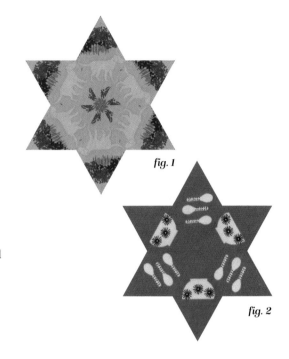

fig. 1

fig. 2

These swatches show the fabric design before being fussy-cut and pieced.

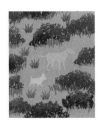

Tips for Design

Give the Eye Room to Rest

It's easy to get swallowed up in wanting to find a fussy-cut for every paper piece you come to. I accidentally fall down this rabbit hole with nearly every project! It's only when I stop to analyze why a design isn't working that I often realize it's because I haven't left any room for the eye to rest.

Using a solid fabric, a simple stripe, or a sprinkling of dots amongst all the wondrous fussy-cutting is a great way to diffuse intensity and allow your work to truly shine.

Coordinating Fabrics

Here are some things I keep in mind when choosing colors and prints:

- As this page demonstrates, use a mix of busy and calm prints to give the eye room to rest.
- Don't be afraid to use the same print several times in one project. Repeating the same color or pattern can often pull a piece together visually. You can also cut the print in different ways to provide interest.
- Black or dark blue are great alternatives to using white. Their visual weight seems to make bright colors placed next to them pop. They can also lend sophistication to a palette that feels overly "girly" in pinks or pastels.
- It's easy to fall into the trap of choosing fabrics solely for their fussy-cutting potential. Try to remember that it's also important that they make your heart soar.
- When first gathering fabrics for a project, start with a print that delights you. Use this favorite print as a springboard and gather fabrics in colors that feature prominently within it. Next, choose fabrics in colors that feature more subtly in that initial print or that feature heavily in the second round of fabrics. Gather more fabrics than you need and edit on the basis of how they hang together and fussy-cutting potential.
- When you're working instinctively, go with it. When you have been analyzing decisions and focusing on a particular aspect intensively, be sure to stand back and look at the bigger picture before committing to your choice.

Above: With no room for the eye to rest, this block looks overwhelmingly intense. **Below:** By swapping just two of the fabrics for something simpler, the main prints have been given more of a chance to shine.

Buying Fabric for Fussy-Cutting

You may start to view your stash of fabric with a different eye when you're considering what you might like to fussy-cut. Here are some of the criteria that I keep in my head when buying fabric for this purpose:

- Geometric designs often have more obvious symmetrical fussy-cuts within them.
- Designs with clearly defined borders can make more impactful and obvious fussy-cuts.
- Large painterly prints can be beautiful, but they offer less distinct fussy-cutting opportunities and can often have large print repeats making it tricky to find identical fussy-cuts across a small piece of fabric.
- Designs with lines, stripes, or banding often make excellent cuts.
- Small-scale designs with a frequent fabric repeat are an economical way to buy fussy-cutting fabrics.
- Larger scale designs are often lost on 1" (2.5 cm) shapes.
- For several years, I stuck to frugally buying quilting fabrics only in fat or skinny quarters. Switching to half-yards has opened up many more options for fussy-cutting, even if my wallet is a little lighter for it.

autHor tip

Fussy-Cutting Favorites: As a jumping-off point, here are four fabric designers who frequently put out beautiful designs that work well for fussy-cutting:

Rashida Coleman-Hale (*cottonandsteelfabrics.com*)

Elizabeth Olwen (*elizabetholwen.com*)

Tula Pink (*tulapink.com*)

Anna Maria Horner (*annamariahorner.com*)

But don't stop at these—you'll quickly discover your own favorites to work with!

CHAPTER FOUR

THE ROSETTES

WHILE THE LINE drawing of a rosette pattern may show clearly defined shapes, it's always fascinating to see how fabric use creates visual illusions that play with those forms. Through our choice of colors, cut, and placement of prints, the same rosette can be reborn in many different incarnations.

Over the following pages, I have detailed the best order to piece together the featured rosettes. Each pattern is shown in different combinations of fabric and includes pointers for pulling together fabrics.

The rosettes in this book can be used however you wish. Make one to frame or to appliqué onto a cushion, or create several identical rosettes that you can sew together to create a mini-quilt or larger-size bedspread. You can use the same prints for each repetition of the rosette or vary the fabric designs you feature in each version.

It's worth noting that the rosettes named Holmwood and Pyegreave produce the same overall size of finished hexagon and can be combined together in a quilt. Billilla, however, is slightly larger and is best used alone or placed in repeat with itself.

Each rosette is named after a place from my childhood.

tips for making rosettes

- The following pages contain suggestions for the best construction order for each rosette. It's important to wrap pieces the right way so shapes fit together properly. Always wrap each piece so the printer ink is visible on the reverse of the shape when wrapped.

- You can find all of the paper shapes needed to make the featured rosettes here: **www.quiltingcompany.com/ FlossieTeacakesTemplates**. Print them at 100% size, with no page-scaling options checked.

- These printable shapes can be cut out and wrapped with fabric. Be sure to cut all fabric with a ¼" (6 mm) seam allowance added on.

- For a helping hand with any aspect, from creating templates for fabric-cutting to sewing with a whipstitch, please consult the extensive techniques section in chapter 3.

HOLMWOOD ROSETTE

My first memories are from our house in Holmwood, Surrey: Making rose perfume with my sister, lying on the bottom bunk as we chatted before sleep, shelves heavy with vinyl and our ears filled with the warm crackle of the record player. In my memory, the days in Holmwood were bathed in sunshine or blanketed in snow, and the house was always warm with the constant flow of family friends who stayed for weeks at a time.

Finished hexagon sides: about 5" (12.5 cm)
Height: about 10" (25.5 cm)
Width: about 8⅝" (22 cm)

NOTE: *Please refer to the Tips for Making Rosettes at the start of this chapter before beginning.*

1 Using a whipstitch and tackling one seam at a time, sew 6 B pieces to the central A piece **(Figure 1)**. Set aside. **NOTE:** *Illustrations show the front of the rosette.*

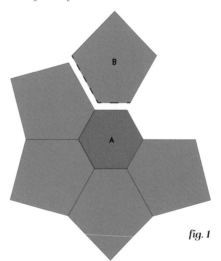

fig. 1

2 Sew 6 pairs of C1 and C2 pieces together and 6 pairs of D1 and D2 pieces together to create the units shown in **Figure 2**. When viewed from the reverse, the numbering will be in the *opposite* order: D2, D1 and C2, C1.

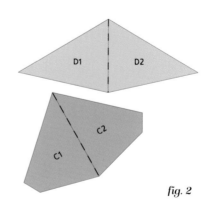

fig. 2

3 Sew the C units to the central A/B flower as shown (**Figure 3**).

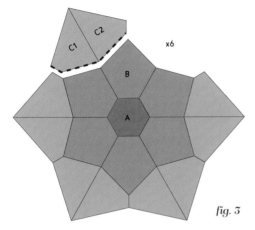

fig. 3

4 Sew on the D units (**Figure 4**) to complete the rosette (**Figure 5**).

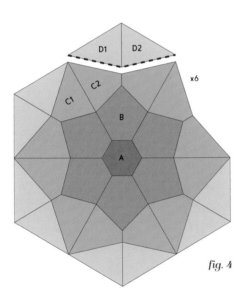

fig. 4

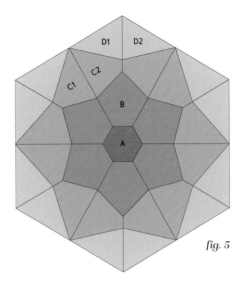

fig. 5

Fussy-cut Holmwood Rosette

Pairs of acrobats circle through the air against the white dotted background, which gives the eyes room to rest. The outer rounds echo the colors of the leotards and gloves to give a cohesive color scheme.

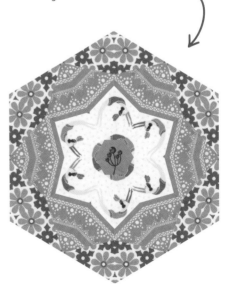

PYEGREAVE ROSETTE

For most of my childhood, my paternal grand-parents lived on Pyegreave Farm (pronounced pie-grieve), surrounded by rolling green hills, in the north of England. Set down a long, bumpy track, the unheated farmhouse was a place of long, mysterious flagstone corridors, loud ticking clocks, a crackling coal fire, sheepdogs barking as visitors arrived in the farmyard, and the rustle of sweets dispensed from my grandmother's sideboard in the hall.

Finished hexagon sides: about 5" (12.5 cm)
Height: about 10" (25.5 cm)
Width: about 8⅝" (22 cm)

NOTE: *Please refer to the Tips for Making Rosettes at the start of this chapter before beginning.*

1 Using a whipstitch, sew a set of B1 and B2 pieces together, joining them at the longer of the two short sides (**Figure 1**). Make 6 B1/B2 units. **NOTE:** *These illustrations show the front of the rosette. When viewed from the reverse, the numbering will be in the opposite order: B2, B1.*

2 Sew each B1/B2 unit to an A piece as shown (**Figure 2**). The goal is to create a smooth edge at each side of this newly formed diamond, so begin sewing at the outer edge with points perfectly aligned and work in toward the center—you may need to ease the shape in a little. Repeat on each side. Make 6 units total.

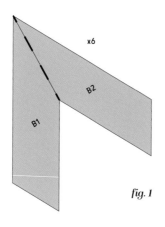

fig. 1

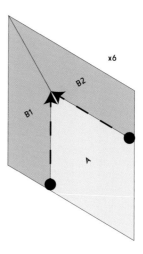

fig. 2

3 Sew 3 A/B units together, aligning intersecting seams (**Figure 3**). Make 2 sets. Once done, sew across the center to create a star, taking care to align the pieces perfectly.

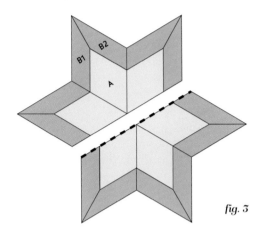

fig. 3

4 Sew 6 C pieces to the A/B star unit as shown (**Figure 4**).

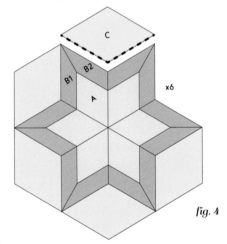

fig. 4

5 Sew together 1 E1, D1, D2, and E2 pieces (**Figure 5**). Make 6 units. **NOTE:** *These illustrations show the front of the rosette. When viewed from the reverse, the numbering will be in the opposite order: E2, D2, D1, E1.*

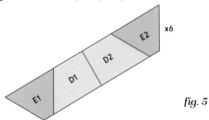

fig. 5

6 Sew each D/E unit to the star unit (**Figure 6**) to complete the rosette (**Figure 7**).

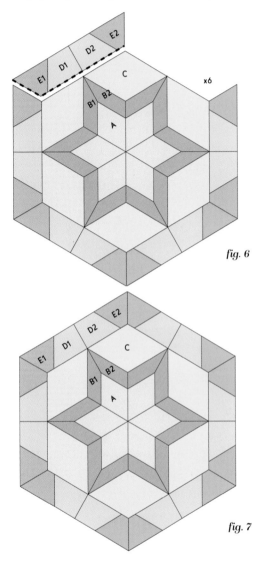

fig. 6

fig. 7

BILLILLa ROSETTE

As a child, my father's work took us to live briefly in Brighton, Australia. Our garden there was filled with the sound of cicadas, water sprinklers, and the squeaking springs of the trampoline upon which my sister and I endlessly bounced. At the end of our unassuming residential street was an oddly placed beautiful white mansion, named Billilla. I fell in love with the building and its manicured lawns, which I longed to play on whenever we walked by.

Finished hexagon sides: about 5½" (14 cm)
Height: about 11" (28 cm)
Width: about 9½" (24 cm)
NOTE: *Please refer to the Tips for Making Rosettes at the start of this chapter before beginning.*

1 Using a whipstitch, sew 3 A pieces together. Make 2 units (**Figure 1**). Join the units across the center line to create a six-pointed shape.

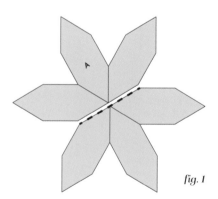

fig. 1

2 Sew 6 B pieces to the six-pointed shape as shown (**Figure 2**).

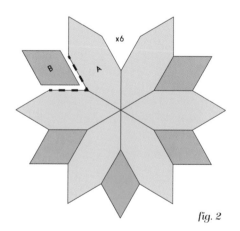

fig. 2

3 Sew 12 C pieces to the A/B unit (**Figure 3**).

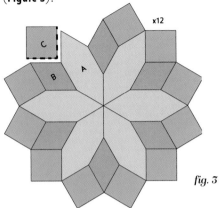

fig. 3

4 Sew a D piece to each set of C squares (**Figure 4**).

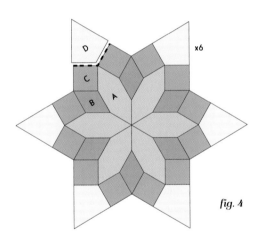

fig. 4

5 Sew a set of F1 and F2 pieces together (**Figure 5**). Make 6 F1/F2 units. These pattern pieces have been supplied as mirror images so they'll be the correct way around once wrapped. Be sure to wrap with the printed line facing the seam allowance and the letter visible on the reverse of the shape once wrapped.

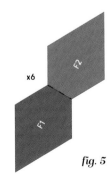

fig. 5

6 Sew 1 E and 1 G piece to each F1/F2 unit as shown to create a large diamond (**Figure 6**).

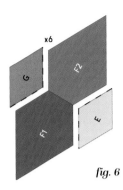

fig. 6

7 Sew these diamond-shaped units to the larger unit (**Figure 7**) to complete the rosette (**Figure 8**).

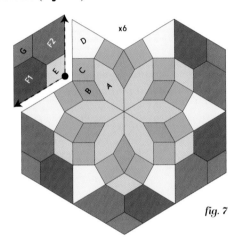

fig. 7

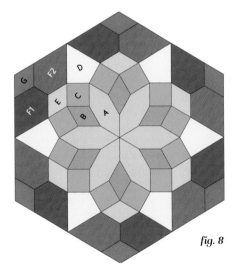

fig. 8

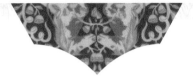

CHAPTER FIVE

THE RIPPLE EFFECT QUILT

I NAMED THIS quilt The Ripple Effect because the rounds of the central rosette remind me of the ripples that expand out over the water surface when a stone is dropped in a pond. It's a sight I've always found mesmerizing. Looking into a pond, I enjoy seeing reflections momentarily disturbed by the flicker of a fish's shimmering body coming into view before it disappears back into the depths. Or studying the miracle of a pond skater walking on water, its legs perfectly poised to exploit the water's surface tension. It always amazes me that its presence makes only the slightest of dimples and ripples on the surface as it scuds by.

The surface of a body of water seems a fascinating, almost indefinable place where two worlds meet. In many ways that reflects the ideas around a quilt discussed in Quilt Tales in chapter 2, where one sees the finished quilt, but only a whisper of the stories that lie beneath, which I imagine to have been absorbed into the fibers as it was being made.

I've designed the central rosette to include several unconventional shapes that you may not have come across already when English paper piecing—there's an exciting challenge in tackling new shapes and a satisfaction in discovering how the pieces slot together. There are even some curves (for tips, see Wrapping Curves and Sewing Curves in chapter 3).

This may be a tricky pattern for a beginner. But when it comes to sewing, I've always enjoyed attempting a stumbling gallop rather

than a sensible trot. Venturing in this way also tends to teach a huge amount and progress one's skill-level in giant show-jumping leaps.

Everything from the central medallion to the outer squares are English paper pieced in this pattern, but there's no reason why you can't machine piece an alternate design to sit around the central medallion if you'd like to finish more quickly. Or, if you prefer hexagons, there's no reason to stick to squares for the outer quadrants. Go wild and enjoy making this pattern your own.

Fabric Notes

Fabric requirements for any English paper pieced quilt are tricky to give because they are dependent on how many different fabrics you choose to include and how you fussy-cut that fabric. While some fabrics may yield eight fussy-cut parts of the central star from less than a fat eighth, others may have a print that is on such a large scale you need a whole yard to gain eight usable repeats. I recommend choosing fabrics for just the first three or four "rounds" of the main rosette, then raiding your stash or buying fabric little and often as you build up the rest of the rosette (depending on what is needed to get a good balance of color with interesting fussy-cuts). The outer quarters of the quilt, where the color graduates from pink to dark blue, were created entirely from tiny scraps in my fabric stash to give a wide variety of prints and shades.

FINISHED QUILT TOP:
60" (152.5 cm) square

TOOLS AND MATERIALS

Fabric for fussy-cutting
(see Fabric Notes)

Background fabric on which to
appliqué the central rosette,
39" (99 cm) square. **NOTE:**
*Because this square will be
placed at a 45-degree angle,
a solid or nondirectional print
fabric works best.*

Thread for English paper piecing

Handsewing needles

½" (1.3 cm) wide bias tape or
ribbon, 88" (223.5 cm) length;
cut into 4 even sections for the
strips surrounding the central
medallion. **NOTE:** *If you're using
self-made bias tape, working with
the straight grain of the fabric is
just as good as the bias grain.*

Tools for basting (either glue
or handsewing; see chapter 3
for directions)

Appliqué glue

Pins for temporarily
securing appliqué pieces

Rotary cutter

Self-healing mat

Small thread scissors

Paper-cutting scissors

Thimble for appliqué (optional)

Paper and a printer for
printing the paper pieces

Template plastic (optional)

The Ripple Effect templates

Before You Begin

Take a moment to read through these important tips for
quilt construction before beginning your quilt top.

- All the paper pieces needed to complete this pattern
  can be downloaded at *www.quiltingcompany.com/
  FlossieTeacakesTemplates*. Be sure to print them
  out at 100% with no page-scaling options.

- Cut and wrap the pieces with care to allow the pattern
  to come together perfectly.

- Piecing the C and D pieces together may be challenging if you're new to EPP. To make things easier, cut out
  and wrap C/D as one piece for step 3.

- As noted elsewhere, any asymmetrical pieces are
  provided as mirror images, so once wrapped (with
  the lettering visible on the back of the shape) they will
  be the correct way around in the finished quilt top.
  Illustrations and lettering are shown as though viewing
  the quilt from the front. For example, the illustrations
  show the front of the quilt top, so what appears as D1,
  D2 in **Figure 6** will read as D2, D1 on the reverse side.

Instructions

1 Sew together 4 A pieces. Make 2 units **(Figure 1)**. Sew the halves together along the long edge.

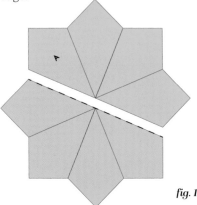

fig. 1

2 Sew 8 B pieces to the A unit as shown **(Figure 2)**.

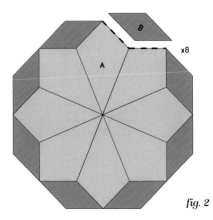

fig. 2

3 Sew together a D1 and D2 piece, joining them along the shortest vertical edge **(Figure 3)**. Make 8 D1/D2 units total.

NOTE: *If you're a beginner or would like to simplify the pattern, see the note in the Quilt Construction Tips about cutting out and wrapping C/D as one piece, then move on to step 5.*

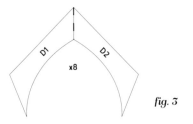

fig. 3

4 Sew 1 C piece inside each D1/D2 unit. To begin, place 1 C piece at the inside point of a D1/D2 unit **(Figure 4)**, with right sides together. Sew out to each side in turn, adjusting the pieces as you go to align a little more of the curve to be sewn each time **(Figure 5)**. Make 8 C/D units total.

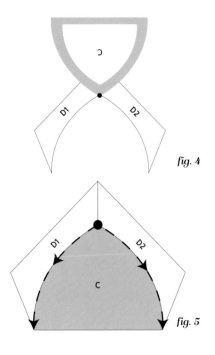

fig. 4

fig. 5

NOTES: *The D pieces taper to a fine point, which can be tricky to detect when wrapping with fabric. The easiest way*

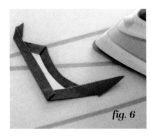

fig. 6

to tackle the D pieces is to wrap the three straight sides and then press the semi-wrapped shape with an iron. This helps the crease of the fabric on the longest of the two short sides to be remembered, so the end of the paper shape is not twisted or cut off when you fold in the curved seam allowance **(Figure 6)**. *Once wrapped, check that all D pieces are identical. It's worth resolving any disparity between pieces at this point to avoid using a seam ripper when placing them in a round later!*

5 Sew 1 C/D unit to the A/B unit and the straight sides of the D units to each other **(Figure 7)**. Sew the remaining C/D units to the A/B units as shown **(Figure 8)**.

6 Sew 8 E pieces to the rosette **(Figure 9)**.

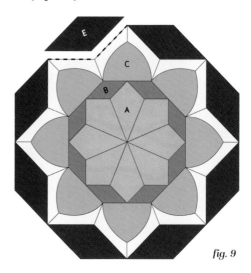

fig. 9

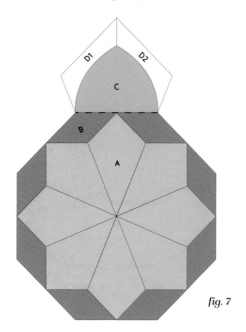

fig. 7

7 Sew an F, G1, and G2 piece together **(Figure 10)**. Make 8 F/G units total. **NOTE:** *Viewed from the reverse, the pieces will read G2, G1, F from left to right.*

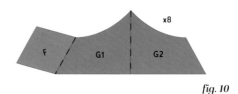

fig. 10

8 Sew an H1a and an H1b piece together. Repeat for pieces H2a and H2b. Sew the combined H1 unit to the combined H2 unit **(Figure 11)**. Make 8 units total. **NOTE:** *Viewed from the reverse, the pieces will read H2a, H2b, H1b, H1a from left to right.*

fig. 8

fig. 11

9 Referring to **Figure 12**, sew the F/G units to the H units, starting at the point indicated by the dot and sewing out to each side. Create 8 of these units.

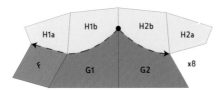

fig. 12

10 Sew one of the units to the rosette as shown **(Figure 13)**. Continue adding these units as shown **(Figure 14)**.

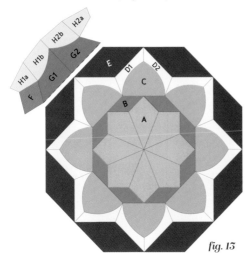

fig. 13

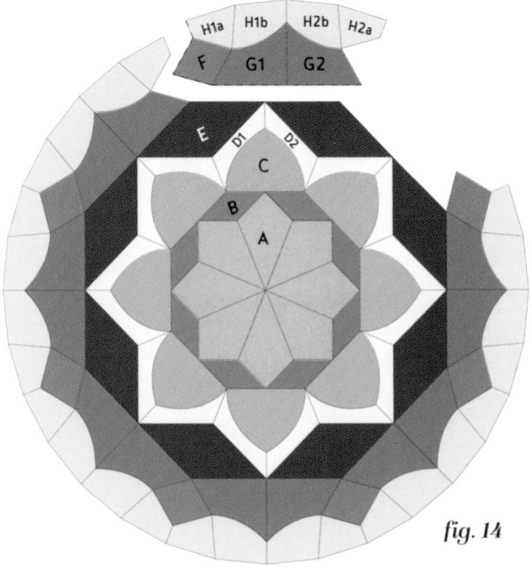

fig. 14

11 Sew 4 K pieces to 4 J pieces **(Figure 15)**. Make 8 K/J units total.

fig. 15

12 Sew the J/K units to the rosette as shown **(Figure 16)**.

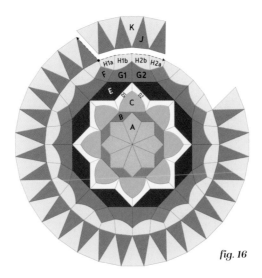

fig. 16

13 Referring to **Figure 17**, sew 4 L pieces together. Make 8 L units total. Then sew 2 M1 units and 2 M2 units together as shown. Make 8 M1/M2 units total. **NOTE:** *Viewed from the reverse, the M pieces will read M1, M2, M1, M2 from left to right.*

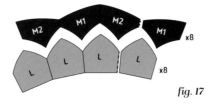

fig. 17

14 Join each L unit to an M1/M2 unit, starting at the point denoted by the dot and working out to each side in turn as shown by the arrows **(Figure 18)**. Make 8 M/L units.

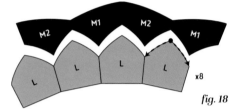

fig. 18

15 Join the L/M units to the rosette **(Figure 19)** to complete the central rosette.

fig. 19

16 Starting with a Q piece, sew together 8 Q pieces and 7 R pieces, alternating Q and R as shown **(Figure 20)**. Make 4 Q/R arc units total. (These will be appliquéd to the same background fabric as the rosette.) Set aside.

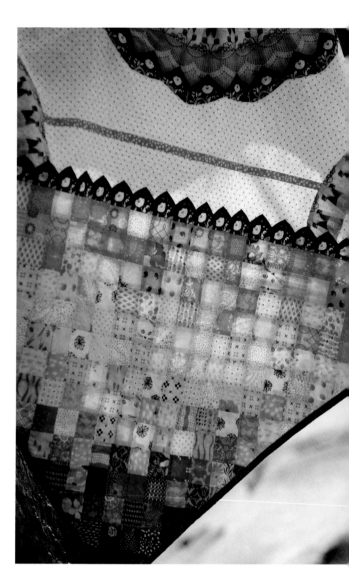

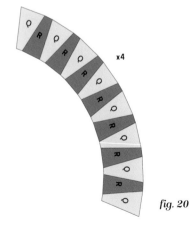

fig. 20

17 Sew together 24 N pieces, then sew 1 N1 piece at the right-hand end **(Figure 21)**. Make 4 units. Set aside.

fig. 21

18 The outer quarters of the quilt are made by English paper piecing hundreds of squares and triangles. Referring to **Figure 22**, sew the required number of O and P pieces together per row to make each outer quarter of the quilt. Make 4 outer quarters total. **NOTE:** *The illustration shows how many squares make up each row and where to place an additional triangle piece at the end of a row. It's also a useful guide if you're considering making a color transition across these outer borders.*

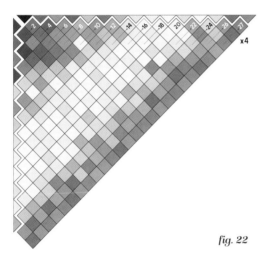

fig. 22

19 Sew 1 N/N1 unit (from step 17) to each outer quarter unit **(Figure 23)**. Study the diagram so the N/N1 unit is placed correctly—this is important to ensure the four quarters fit together perfectly later. N1 should always be at the far left-hand side.

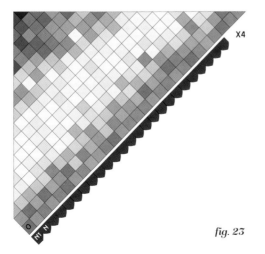

fig. 23

20 Carefully sew the outer quarters together. I found it easiest to sew the side of N and N1 together and then move around the corner to sew the remaining squares to one another. Once completed, move on to attach the next quadrant in the same way. Working in a clockwise direction may add some orderliness to proceedings. This is a most unwieldy task, but thankfully it is over relatively quickly!

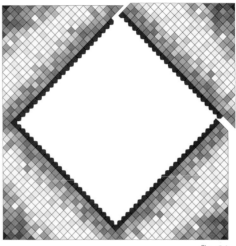

fig. 24

21 Press the quilt top with an iron. Gently remove all the papers, being careful to retain the curved edge of the N pieces. This is a simple task if you favor thread-basting. For glue-basted pieces, I recommend unwrapping the straight edges first, then gently teasing back the curved seam allowances. Holding the tip where the two curved edges meet helps ensure the curved shape is perfectly retained when finally removing the paper. Press the top again.

22 Fold the 39" (99 cm) square of fabric in half diagonally to create a triangle, then fold it diagonally in half again and finger-press the folds to create visible creases. (You'll use these creases as a visual guide later.)

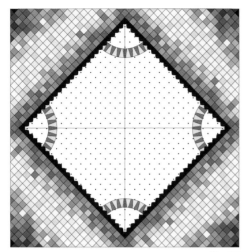

fig. 25

NOTE: *Refer to Figure 25 for steps 23 and 24.*

23 Place the background fabric square at a 45-degree angle behind the joined outer quarters—it's easy to place the fabric centrally by peeking at the back. (The square should rest exactly on the straight horizontal edge of the N units.) Pin the square in place but don't use any appliqué glue quite yet.

24 Remove the papers from the Q/R arc units, press, and turn the dogs' ears under. Press again. Place the Q/R arc units in the corners of the square with the central R piece in each arc on the crease. Slip each end of the arc unit under the tip of the 6th N piece (not counting the corner N1 piece).

fig. 26

NOTE: *Refer to 26 for steps 25 and 26.*

25 Glue or pin each N row and each Q/R arc unit into place, leaving a small section around the outer edge of the second R piece on each side unbasted to accommodate the ends of the strips of tape or ribbon. Appliqué the pieces in place, matching the thread color to the piecing.

26 Place the 4 strips of tape or ribbon, tucking the ends under the second R piece at each side of the arc. Pin the strips in place, being sure each strip is as level as possible between the two points. Appliqué in place using thread to match the strip, then sew the remaining portions of the arc units.

27 Remove the papers from the central medallion and press with an iron, turning any dogs' ears under. Center the medallion in the center of the quilt top—use the creases you created earlier as a guide. Pin in place, then glue baste the outer edge to the base cloth. Appliqué in place **(Figure 27)**.

fig. 27

Congratulations! Your quilt top is now finished and ready for you to turn into a quilt or coverlet.

Acknowledgments

Appreciative thanks to Amelia Johanson and Stephanie White; Robert Wake at York Museum Trust; Todd Purcell at Superior Threads; Diana Boston of Hemingford Grey Manor; Julia Hedgecoe; Sarah Wasley; Ruth Battersby Tooke, Norwich Castle Study Centre; Heather Audin at The British Quilt Guild; Bridget Long; Katy Emck, Katie Steingold, and Caroline Wilkinson of Fine Cell Work; Kathleen Burke at NGV; Janene Ford; Ashley Kath-Bilsky; Stephen Garcia, University of Michigan; Robert Sill & Doug Carr, Illinois State Museum; Liz Smith; Tommy Hatwell Photography; Tracy Chevalier, for happily agreeing to appear in this book; my contributors, who generously shared snapshots of their lives and quilts; the people whose research and ideas I cited—I truly hope I reflected your work accurately; Roddy Paine and Gavin Sawyer for their wonderful photography; everyone at F+W; Pamela Norman, for putting this book together with such wonderful creativity, flair, and thoughtfulness; Debra Fehr Greenway for her eagle eyes; and Jodi Butler, for being a delight to work with, peppering her feedback with reassuring smiley faces, and holding her editorial toothcomb in a nonscary way.

Love and thanks to my friends, for the fun and encouragement they offered whenever I emerged from the attic; Kathryn, for always saying "go for it" and without whom there would be no attic; Laura, for contract advice, sisterhood, and filling my head with perfect nuggets of reassurance; Mama, for looking over my writing with love and enthusiasm and making invaluable suggestions; Popsie, for right-hand-manning and a joyful dedication to moving immovable objects; Matilda and Finn, for being two of the best human beings I know—this book came to life, in no small part, because of their encouragement, kindness, generosity and enthusiasm—I am so very grateful; Ian, for never letting me fall, attempting to attach wings to my back at every opportunity, affectionately tolerating my odd ways and making my stomach ache from laughter with the Austrian EPP sensations, Klaus and Svetty Hans, whose idiosyncratic approach to quilt-making is a delight. Thank you for everything.

Warmest thanks to my blog readers and fellow stitchers for the enthusiasm, friendship, and thoughtful conversation offered over the last decade.

Finally, special thanks to the following fabric designers, whose beautiful fabrics feature in some of the patchwork page borders and on the cover: Elizabeth Olwen, Alexia Abegg, Sarah Watts, Bari J, Karen Lewis, Brigitte Heitland of Zen Chic, Lizzy House, Kaffe Fassett, Emily Herrick, Liberty London, Sarah Watson, Pat Bravo, Tone Finnanger (of Tilda), and Annabel Wrigley.

Bibliography/References

A BRIEF HISTORY: Audin, Heather. *Patchwork and Quilting in Britain.* Oxford: Shire Publications, 2013. • Briscoe, Susan. *The 1718 Coverlet: 69 Quilt Blocks from the Oldest Dated British Patchwork Coverlet.* David & Charles, 2014. • Gero, Annette, and Katie Somerville. *Making the Australian Quilt: 1800-1950.* Melbourne: Victoria National Gallery of Victoria, 2016. • Long, Bridget. "Anonymous Needlework: Uncovering British Patchwork 1680-1820." PhD diss., University of Hertfordshire, 2014. http://hdl.handle.net/2299/15367. • Pritchard, Sue, ed. *Quilts, 1700-2010: Hidden Histories, Untold Stories.* London: V&A Publishing, 2010. Online source: http://collections.vam.ac.uk/item/O14716/patchwork-quilt-unknown/. • Sheppard, Josie. *Through the Needle's Eye: The Patchwork and Quilt Collection at York Castle Museum.* York Museum Trust, 2005.

FABRIC AND LANGUAGE SOURCES: Collier, Ann Futterman. *Using Textile Arts and Handcrafts in Therapy with Women: Weaving Lives Back Together.* London: Jessica Kingsley Publishers, 2012. • Farlex. *The Free Dictionary,* Idioms tab: http://idioms.thefreedictionary.com/. • Feynman, Richard. "The Law of Gravitation, an Example of Physical Law." 1964 Messenger Lectures at Cornell University video, 55:25. November 9-19, 1964. www.cornell.edu/video/richard-feynman-messenger-lecture-1-law-of-gravitation. • Genesis 3:7 (Authorized [King James] Version). • Long, Bridget. "Anonymous Needlework: Uncovering British Patchwork 1680-1820." PhD diss., University of Hertfordshire, 2014. http://hdl.handle.net/2299/15367. • Razzall, Lucy, and Jason Scott-Warren (organizers). *2012 Texts & Textiles Conference,* University of Cambridge. www.english.cam.ac.uk/cmt/?page_id=2630.

WORKING WITH OUR HANDS: Buchholz, Ester Schaler. *The Call of Solitude: Alonetime in a World of Attachment.* Riverside, New Jersey: Simon & Schuster, 2000. • Collier, Ann Futterman. *Using Textile Arts and Handcrafts in Therapy with Women: Weaving Lives Back Together,* p. 53. London: Jessica Kingsley Publishers, 2012. • Corkhill, Betsan. *Knit for Health & Wellness: How to Knit a Flexible Mind & More...* Bath, UK: FlatBear Publishing, 2014. • Csikszentmihalyi, Mihaly. *Flow: The Classic Work on how to Achieve Happiness.* Rider, 2002. • Hammond, Claudia. "How Being Alone May be the Key to Rest," *BBC Magazine* (September 27, 2016). www.bbc.com/news/magazine-37444982. • Klerman, Gerald L., and Myrna M. Weissman. "Increasing Rates of Depression." *JAMA* 261, no. 15 (April 21, 1989): 2229-2235.doi:10.1001/jama.1989.03420150079041. • Lambert, Kelly. *Lifting Depression: A Neuroscientist's Hands-On Approach to Activating Your Brain's Healing Power* (antidepressant effectiveness, p. 6; rates of depression, p. 26; complex cortex, p. 33; emotionally drained brain, p. 74; therapeutic intervention, p. 90; repetitive movement in farm animals, p. 109). New York: Basic Books, 2008. • Mark Lacas, CEO of Dataprism, quoted in Frances Booth, *The Distraction Trap: How to Focus in a Digital World,* (Harlow, England: Pearson, 2013). • McKay, Sarah. "Why Crafting Is Great For Your Brain: A Neuroscientist Explains." mindbodygreen, June 24, 2014. www.mindbodygreen.com/0-14252/why-crafting-is-great-for-your-brain-a-neuroscientist-explains.html. • Reiner, Robert H. Unpublished clinical study commissioned by American Home Sewing & Craft Association (HSA), 1995. • Riley, Jill, Betsan Corkhill, and Clare Morris. "The Benefits of Knitting for Personal and Social Wellbeing in Adulthood: Findings from an International Survey," *British Journal of Occupational Therapy* 76, no. 2 (February, 2013): 50-57.doi:10.4276/030802213X13603244419077. • Tawa, Renee. "Mending Tattered Nerves." *Los Angeles Times,* July 15, 1999. http://articles.latimes.com/1999/jul/15/news/cl-56016.

CREATING ORDER IN CHAOS: Battersby-Tooke, Ruth (curator). *Frayed: Textiles on the Edge.* Time & Tide Museum, Great Yarmouth (October 2013-March 2014). https://frayedtextilesontheedge.wordpress.com/. • Collier, Ann Futterman. *Using Textile Arts and Handcrafts in Therapy with Women: Weaving Lives Back Together,* p. 92. London: Jessica Kingsley Publishers, 2012. • Lambert, Kelly. *Lifting Depression: A Neuroscientist's Hands-On Approach to Activating Your Brain's Healing Power,* pp. 90, 230-231. New York: Basic Books, 2008. • Quakers in the World. "William Tuke." www.quakersintheworld.org/quakers-in-action/93.

THE QUILT IN THE CUPBOARD: Bayles, David, and Ted Orland. *Art & Fear: Observations on the Perils (and Rewards) of Artmaking.* Image Continuum Press, 2001.

FINE CELL WORK: Bell, Robert. *The Rajah Quilt.* National Gallery of Australia, June 2016. • Emck, Katy (founding director of Fine Cell Work), interview with author October 12, 2016. • *Fine Cell Work,* www.finecellwork.co.uk.QA

Research. "Stitching a Future: An Evaluation of Fine Cell Work" (final report, July 2011), www.finecellwork.co.uk/assets/0000/2418/Fine_Cell_Work_evaluation_Short_version.pdf. • Wilkinson, Caroline (Fine Cell Work tutor), interview with author October 18, 2016.

SYMMETRY AND REPEATING PATTERNS: Feng, Charles. "Looking Good: The Psychology and Biology of Beauty," *Journal of Young Investigators* 6, no. 6 (2002). http://legacy.jyi.org/volumes/volume6/issue6/features/feng.html. • Lightman, Alan. *The Accidental Universe: The World You Thought You Knew.* New York: Pantheon Books, 2013. • Little, Anthony C., Benedict C. Jones, and Lisa M. DeBruine. "Facial Attractiveness: Evolutionary Based Research," *Philosophical Transactions of the Royal Society B* 366, no. 1571 (May 2, 2011): 1638-1659. doi:10.1098/rstb.2010.0404. • BBC World Service. "Symmetry," *Discovery*, March 22, 1995. www.bbc.co.uk/programmes/p03jrwf0 (podcast), 29:00. • Wade, David. The Ordering Principal, Wooden Books 2006. • BBC Radio 4. In Our Time, April 2007.

A LIFE'S WORK: Breuning, Loretta Graziano. *Habits of a Happy Brain: Retrain Your Brain to Boost Your Serotonin, Dopamine, Oxytocin, & Endorphin Levels,* Avon, MA: Adams Media, 2016. • Csikszentmihalyi, Mihaly. *Flow: The Classic Work on how to Achieve Happiness,* p. 46. Rider, 2002. • Duckworth, Angela. *Grit: the Power of Passion and Perseverence.* New York: Scribner, 2016. Angela Duckworth's TED Talk, *Grit: the Power of Passion and Perseverence,* www.ted.com/talks/angela_lee_duckworth_grit_the_power_of_passion_and_perseverance . Garcia, Stephen M., and Avishalom Tor. "The *N-Effect*: More Competitors, Less Competition," *Psychological Science* 20, no. 7 (July 1, 2009): 871-877. doi:10.1111/j.1467-9280.2009.02385.x • Garcia, Stephen, email correspondence November 8, 2016 with author • Harkin, Benjamin, et al. "Does Monitoring Goal Progress Promote Goal Attainment? A Meta-Analysis of the Experimental Evidence," *Psychological Bulletin* 142, no. 2 (2016): 198-229. doi:10.1037/bul0000025. • Kaufman, Scott Barry, and Carolyn Gregoire. *Wired to Create: Unraveling the Mysteries of the Creative Mind.* New York: Perigee Books, 2015.

THE QUILTS OF ALBERT SMALL: Illinois State Museum collection notes. • Smith, Liz, telephone interview November 6, 2016 with author.

QUILT TALES: Boston, Diana. *The Patchworks of Lucy Boston,* p. 8. Oldknow Books, 2009. • Chevalier, Tracy, interview January 17, 2017 with author. • Godfrey, Jodi, interview with author November 3, 2016. • Kath-Bilsky, Ashley. "The Graveyard Quilt," *Ashley Kath-Bilsky* (blog). https://ashleykathbilsky.com/2010/09/05/the-graveyard-quilt/.

CONSIDERING DISTRACTIONS: BBC Radio 3. "Hands, Physiology and Art, the History of Science," *Free Thinking* (June 2016). www.bbc.co.uk/programmes/b07gnj18 (podcast), 45:00. • Csikszentmihalyi, Mihaly. "Flow: the Secret to Happiness," Filmed February 2004. TED video, 18:55. www.ted.com/talks/mihaly_csikszentmihalyi_on flow. • Lambert, Kelly. *Lifting Depression: A Neuroscientist's Hands-On Approach to Activating Your Brain's Healing Power,* p. 66. New York: Basic Books, 2008. • Leader, Darian. *Hands: What We Do with Them–and Why,* p. 102. Hamish Hamilton Ltd, 2016.

THE PATCHWORKS OF LUCY BOSTON: Boston, Diana. *The Patchworks of Lucy Boston.* Oldknow Books, 2009. • Boston, Diana, interview with author October 11, 2016.

THE LAST RUNAWAY: Chevalier, Tracy. *The Last Runaway.* New York: Dutton, 2013. • Chevalier, Tracy, interview with author and kind permission to quote from her book January 17, 2017.

METRIC CONVERSION CHART

To Convert	To	Multiply By
Inches	Centimeters	2.54
Centimeters	Inches	0.4
Feet	Centimeters	30.5
Centimeters	Feet	0.03
Yards	Meters	0.9
Meters	Yards	1.1

Index

keep expanding YOUR SKILLS

WITH THESE GREAT TITLES FROM THE QUILTING COMPANY.

THE QUILTER'S PAPER-PIECING WORKBOOK

Paper Piece with Confidence to Create 18 Gorgeous Quilted Projects

Elizabeth Dackson
978-1-63250-180-6 | $25.99

QUILT WITH TULA & ANGELA

A Start-to-Finish Guide to Piecing and Quilting Using Color and Shape

Tula Pink and Angela Walters
978-1-44024-545-9 | $26.99

RED & WHITE QUILTING

An Iconic Tradition in 40 Blocks

Linda Pumphrey
978-1-44024-744-6 | $27.99

WEEKEND QUILTING

Quilt and Unwind with Simple Designs to Sew in No Time

Jemima Flendt
978-1-44024-661-6 | $24.99